YORKSHIR[E]
30 PUB WALKS

Len Markham

COUNTRYSIDE BOOKS
NEWBURY BERKSHIRE

COUNTRYSIDE BOOKS
3 Catherine Road
Newbury, Berkshire

To view our complete range of books,
please visit us at
www.countrysidebooks.co.uk

ISBN 978 1 84674 370 2

Cover photo of Burnsall by Steven Gillis, supplied by Alamy

Designed by KT Designs, St Helens

Produced through The Letterworks Ltd., Reading
Typeset by KT Designs, St Helens
Printed by The Holywell Press, Oxford

CONTENTS

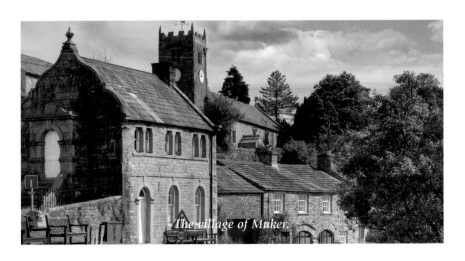

The village of Muker.

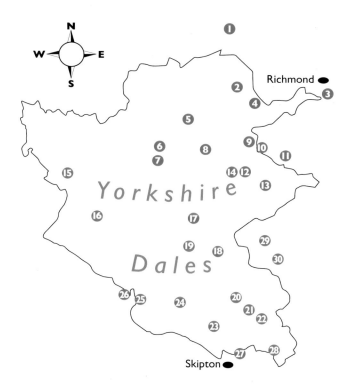

PUBLISHER'S NOTE

We hope that you obtain considerable enjoyment from this book; great care has been taken in its preparation. Although at the time of publication all routes followed public rights of way or permitted paths, diversion orders can be made and permissions withdrawn.

We cannot, of course, be held responsible for such diversion orders or any inaccuracies in the text which result from these or any other changes to the routes, nor any damage which might result from walkers trespassing on private property. We are anxious, though, that all the details covering the walks are kept up to date, and would therefore welcome information from readers which would be relevant to future editions.

The simple sketched maps that accompany the walks in this book are based on notes made by the author whilst surveying the routes on the ground. In order to assist in navigation to the start point of the walk, we have included the nearest postcode, although of course a postcode cannot always deliver you to a precise starting point, especially in rural areas.

However, for the benefit of a proper map, we do recommend that you purchase the relevant Ordnance Survey sheet covering your walk. Ordnance Survey maps are widely available, especially through booksellers and local newsagents.

INTRODUCTION

My first *Pub Walks in the Yorkshire Dales* title, which was published in 2000, came at a time when digital media threatened to relegate the printed word to dusty shelves and libraries, the convenience of satellite navigation and handheld route-finders seemingly consigning books like this to oblivion. But like the Yorkshire sun, this little book rises again, renewed and reinvigorated for a new generation of walkers.

Unlike new technology, this book is companionable, friendly, reliable and is infused with this author's spirit and steadfast love for the tracks and paths of his native county. Pop it in your backpack and enjoy the ride!

The Yorkshire Dales embrace one of the most inspiring landscapes in the whole of the British Isles, encompassing quiet valleys, hills, moorland, woodland and soaring peaks, all intersected by a labyrinth of footpaths and trails to suit every level of fitness. The king of them all is the Pennine Way, a 268-mile marathon along the backbone of England; some of his highness's regal tracks feature in this modest compendium.

None of these walks exceed eight miles in length, and all are circular, enabling ramblers to return to their starting points invigorated but unwearied by distance, their appetites honed for some excellent food in a variety of historic and colourful pubs.

A map, instructions and the details of the relevant pub accompany each walk, along with detailed descriptions of routes, topography, wildlife, ancient monuments and castles, local history and literary figures – some of whom, like James Herriot of *All Creatures Great and Small* fame, have become household names.

As you will gather, I'm wildly passionate about walking, particularly in the Yorkshire Dales.

Len Markham

Bowes Castle

1 BOWES

Distance: 2½ miles / 4 km

Map: OS Landranger 92 / OS Outdoor Leisure 30 GR: NY 995135

How to get there: Bowes is just off the A66 between Scotch Corner and Appleby. The imposing Ancient Unicorn is on the High Street. Sat nav: DL12 9HL.

Parking: Park in the pub car park or on the street.

Once the principal stop on the coaching route between York and Carlisle, Bowes is at the windswept northern boundary of the Yorkshire Dales. Roman legions passed this way, and a castle was built here for Henry II in 1171. This elevated hamlet is not a place to linger in bad weather: searching winds and heavy snowfall intermittently block the A66 trans-Pennine route in winter. But Bowes is a captivating draw for all seekers of the wild frontier. Charles Dickens also travelled here in 1838, drawn by the disreputability of the local schoolmaster William Shaw, who was immortalised as Wackford Squeers in *Nicholas Nickleby*. The unfortunate George Taylor, who inspired the creation of the savagely treated Smike, lies in the churchyard; the grave of his tormentor lies close by.

Our walk follows the Dickens trail (at the western end of the street is a private residence which inspired the notorious Dotheboys Hall), visiting the skeletal remains of the castle and the banks of the River Greta, and passing the therapeutic St Earmin's Well along the way. Atmospheric and totally absorbing, Bowes leaves a lasting impression. **Note:** As the walk involves crossing the Greta on stepping stones, it is not suitable after heavy rain.

St Earmin's Well beside the river Greta

THE PUB THE ANCIENT UNICORN was completely refurbished in 2015, but this 16th-century grey-gabled former coaching inn has lost none of its rustic charms. The sensitive but thoroughly modern restoration provides 12 bedrooms, a bar, a restaurant and an all-day coffee shop serving afternoon teas. Locally produced food and ales are featured on the menu. www.ancientunicorn.com ☎ 01833 628576.

The Walk

❶ Turn right from the inn along the street. At the far end is **Bowes Academy**, alias Dotheboys Hall. Go left between the church and the castle, following the sign to a gate. The inspiration for Squeers – William Shaw, who Dickens met – is buried in the churchyard.

❷ Go through the gate (do not enter the castle enclosure unless visiting) and steer diagonally right over a field to a wall stile. Once over, drop down left over uneven ground towards the river, swing right and look out for a stile to the right. Cross right into a wood, continue above the river crossing to a second stile, and head right following a yellow arrow marker. Drop down into the dip, and veer right across the

flank of the hill for about 400 metres
to find a ladder stile over a
wall next to the lane.
Cross left onto the
lane.

3 Go left and swing
right on the lane.
Go through a
gate, and pass
Swinholme,
dropping down
to the river. Cross
on stepping stones,
and continue to a gate.
Go through and walk
on to the next gate, going left
following the circular walk sign.
Continue on the lane for just under a mile.

4 Go left at the lane junction, and walk on to cross the river bridge.

5 Turn left following the footpath sign, and walk along the river, ignoring the first path to the right. Pass the holy well dedicated to St Earmin, and continue to a stile. Cross, continuing for 200 metres to a marker post, and then go right uphill to retread the outward route. Follow the path to the village, going right to arrive back at the inn.

Places of interest nearby

The **Bowes Museum** (thebowesmuseum.org.uk ☎ 01833 690606), in the market town of Barnard Castle, is just five miles away. Artefacts are housed in a 19th-century French chateau-style pile and include a nationally renowned collection of decorative art, ceramics, textiles, costume, archaeology and local history. There is also a popular café and shop.

Old Gang Smeltmill, near Langthwaite

2 LANGTHWAITE

Distance: 2 miles / 3.2 km

Map: OS Landranger 92 / OS Outdoor Leisure 30 GR: NZ 005025

How to get there: The little-visited Arkengarthdale, an offshoot of Swaledale, is just three miles north-west from Reeth (B6270) along a minor road. Lilliputian Langthwaite is its only settlement. Sat nav: DL11 6RE.

Parking: Apart from the odd space or two, there is no formal parking outside the pub or in Langthwaite. Park in the visitors' car park 200 metres south-east of the village.

Occupying a rocky niche by the enchanting Arkle Beck, Langthwaite could easily fit into Gulliver's palm. Once a thriving centre for lead mining, the area's isolation and tranquillity now beckon walkers and cyclists, who come here to enjoy some of the wildest scenery in Yorkshire.

Beginning by the banks of the Arkle Beck, the walk leads on to the imposing Scar House before crossing meadows and ascending over rough terrain to the old lead mining grounds, the pits, adits and smelt mills which once employed thousands. Today, only the greening spoil heaps and the abandoned hushes and shafts are left.

THE PUB THE RED LION is as diminutive as the rest of Langthwaite. This loveable, cosy urchin of a pub is all cubbyholes and niches, and also serves as a sweetshop and bookstore. The simple menu, available at lunchtime and in the evening, offers pies, pasties, sandwiches and Theakston ales from Masham, the bartop line-up including the infamous Riggwelter. Anyone who has ever encountered an upturned sheep struggling with its legs in the air will know the condition can be fatal! www.langthwaite-redlion.co.uk ☎ 01748 884218.

The Walk

❶ Go left from the pub and left again past **Stone Lea** to a gate. Go through onto the beckside footpath, and follow the well-defined waymarked route over the meadows via a succession of gates and stiles to **Scar House**, arcing left of the house to an access lane and a bridge over the beck. Cross and fork left past **West House Cottage**.

❷ Veer right across the meadow towards the farm cottage, and go through the wall gap into the next meadow, keeping left across the meadow corner to find a second gap in the middle of the wall. Go through and turn immediately right wallside, continuing to a stile. Cross to the right of the cottage, and walk on to the road.

3 Cross the road and follow the footpath sign through a gap in the wall, climbing up on an ill-defined route over tussock grass and aiming to the right of the top cottage. Cross a planked bridge over a drain, and go left at the topmost side of the cottage.

4 Go through two gates and merge with a rough track going through the old ore fields to the road.

5 Keeping the same direction, cross the road and follow the footpath sign for about 300 yards, then follow the path left between the hillocks, heading for the stand of three trees near the cottage. Join the track to the right of the cottage and follow this down, swinging left. Go through a gate to the next fork, and swing left and right, going through twin gates to **Langthwaite**.

Places of interest nearby

Langthwaite's halcyon **St Mary's Church** must be one of the most beautifully situated in the Yorkshire Dales. Approached by a broad avenue of trees from the west, it sits quietly by the Arkle Beck. Spaciously built in 1818 to receive legions of lead miners, it could today accommodate the entire population of the hamlet a hundred times over. Also worth visiting is the **Charles Bathurst Inn**, named after a local mine owner, which is ¾ mile up the valley. The profits of mining were substantial: Bathurst built the imposing King's Head Hotel in Richmond (see Walk 3).

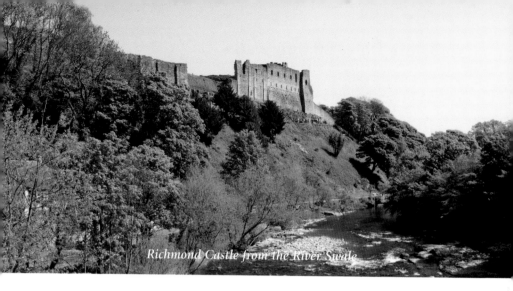

Richmond Castle from the River Swale

3 RICHMOND

Distance: 1½ miles / 2.4 km

Map: OS Landranger 92 / OS Outdoor Leisure 30 GR: NZ 172009

How to get there: Richmond is the ancient gateway to Swaledale and is easily reached from the A1 via the A6108 or the B6271. Sat nav: DL10 4UW or DL10 4DW.

Parking: Park in one of the conveniently situated pay and display car parks in the town centre.

Dramatically placed on an escarpment above the picturesque River Swale, Richmond grew up around the battlements of its castle. Guarded by steep cliffs and a series of narrow, labyrinthine bar gates, the citadel, which dates from 1071, rears up like a defending sword, casting an enchanting spell on its town.

Beginning in the shadow of the old battlements, this historic saunter probes the old defences, taking you along the narrow alleyways – or *wynds*, as they are known locally – and on, through church grounds, to a park by the river. The walk culminates in a climb on the curtain walls.

THE PUB

THE KING'S HEAD is centrally placed in Richmond's imposing market square. Elegant and sophisticated, this 24-bedroom hotel has recently been refurbished; its excellent attractions now include a fashionable coffee shop, a patisserie, a restaurant and bars serving fresh and innovatively presented local produce. Previous guests at this 18th-century coaching inn, which was purpose-built as an exclusive hotel, include the composer Franz Liszt and the painter William Turner, who used it as a base for his sketchbook wanderings along the nearby River Swale. www.kingsheadrichmond. co.uk ☎ 01748 850220.

The Walk

❶ Turn left from the hotel, and take the next left down **Frenchgate**. The master of Richmond School, James Tate, lived in Swale House. The young scholar Lewis Carroll also had lodgings here. On the left is another interesting old house – **Grove House**. Built in then-fashionable brick in 1750, it was the home of Caleb Readshaw, who made his money by exporting knitted woollen caps and stockings to the Low Countries. Continue along Frenchgate, passing the house where Robert Willance once lived. In 1606, whilst out riding, this gentleman plunged over a steep cliff upstream of Richmond. His horse died, but he survived. The cliff on Whitcliffe Scar has since been known as Willance's Leap. Turn right down **Church Wynd**.

❷ Enter the churchyard on a path; go next left and leave the churchyard, turning right through a gate. Go right again on **Lombards Wynd** to the road. Cross the road and go straight ahead into the park.

❸ Swing right on a broad footway above the river, following the path right and left and continuing on **Park Wynd**. Turn right up the hill for 20 metres, and walk up the narrow steps to **Castle Walk** beneath the castle. Legend has it that a local man, Potter Thompson, discovered a cave beneath the castle. Inside he found King Arthur and his knights sleeping soundly. They slumber on until a time when England may need their help. Swing right below the castle. Continue to the last bench before the bollards, and go left down a narrow wynd to the bar. This was built in 1320. From this eminence you can see the tall,

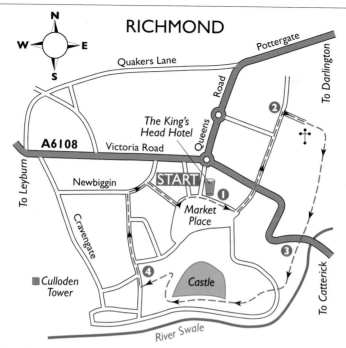

distinctive, octagonal Culloden Tower, erected in 1746 to rejoice in the Jacobite defeat. Go left under the bar down **Cornforth Hill**.

4 Turn right and walk up the steep **Bargate** to the top; go right on **Rosemary Lane** and right again down **Finkle Street**. There was another bar located near the Black Lion, but it was demolished in 1773. Continue back to the market place and the hotel.

Places of interest nearby

In addition to the magnificently sited castle, Richmond has many attractions. There are three museums in the town: the **Green Howards Museum**, displaying regimental history and memorabilia (www.greenhowards.org.uk ☎ 01748 826561); the **Richmondshire Museum**, dedicated to local life and industries (www.richmondshiremuseum.org.uk ☎ 01748 825611); and the **Georgian Theatre Royal Museum**, one of the oldest surviving theatres in the UK, which displays theatre history (www.georgiantheatreroyal.co.uk ☎ 01748 825252).

The village of Reeth

4 REETH

Distance: 3 miles / 4.8 km

Map: OS Landranger 98 / OS Outdoor Leisure 30 GR: SE 038993

How to get there: Reeth is west of Richmond on the B6270.
Sat nav: DL11 6SY.

Parking: Park on or around the extensive green (voluntary contributions for upkeep).

Reeth, the capital of Swaledale, is a fine market town with an independent air and solid, unpretentious stone houses encircling an expansive green. It sits confidently in the prong of the Swale and the Arkle Beck, with a curving backdrop of hills with names like Carver, High Carl, High Harker and Great Pinseat. In 1934, Reeth was described by Ella Pontefract as 'a little country in itself ... once there shut in by barriers of hills you are satisfied and shrouded in its mystery and the rest of the world seems unimportant and unreal.' In almost 85 years it has hardly changed.

This stroll from the green takes you down to the banks of the Swale. Crossing on a footbridge, the route follows the river down to Grinton, where you can visit the ancient church of St Andrew. The return track is over water meadows beside the Arkle Beck.

THE PUB

THE KINGS ARMS dates from 1734, its gaping inglenook fire still blazing a welcome after nearly 300 years. Known locally as the 'Middle House', referring to its central position on the green, the hotel offers a relaxed and typically bluff Yorkshire atmosphere, providing fine accommodation, hearty meals and locally brewed ale. Sunday roasts are resoundingly popular.
www.thekingsarms.com ☎ 01748 884259.

The Walk

1 Swing right from the inn and then right again down the alley, following the sign to the river. Continue on a narrow pathway, walking between the bungalows, and turn left. Take the next right, following the sign to the swing bridge. Continue on the raised flagged walkway and then on a rough track for 40 metres, before turning left downhill on a path between two walls to a gate. Go through and arc right, away from the river, on a footpath continuing to the footbridge. Cross left over the river, and continue slightly left for about 300 metres to the **Harkerside** direction sign.

2 Turn left along the level ground, and continue to the wicket gate. Go through, and keep going in the same direction fenceside at the bottom of the field, going left through a gate on a path wallside. Go through a gate and swing right between broken walls on a stony track to the next gate. Go through and walk on by the river, swinging right away from the bank through a gate to a quiet lane. Turn left, and at the churchyard boundary, go left, following the footpath sign through a gap in the wall, swinging right beside the river to **Grinton. St Andrew's Church**, to the right, was built by the monks of Bridlington 900 years ago. It has many treasures, including the hagioscope, the 14th-century carved font cover and the Jacobean pulpit.

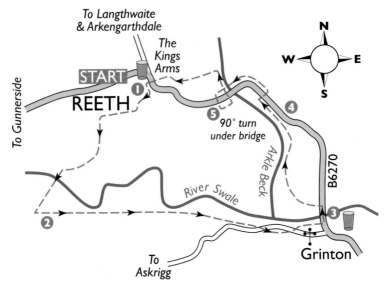

3 Turn left on the footway past the **Bridge Inn** and cross **Grinton Bridge**; then turn immediately left, following a footpath sign through a wall gap and a gate to a meadow. Go through the kissing gate, and keep diagonally right across the second meadow, arcing right towards the barn and going left of it. Go through a gate, following the footpath sign to Reeth, and continue to the road.

4 Go left using the footway to **Reeth Bridge**, and cross.

5 Turn immediately sharp left, going left again under the arch of the bridge along the beck footpath. Take the next left through two gates, following a footpath over a field; then go right between narrow walls and then left past the cottages back into **Reeth**.

Places of interest nearby

Near the end of the walk is the **Swaledale Museum** (www.swaledalemuseum.org ☎ 01748 884118), featuring 'over 270 million years of local history'. There are fascinating displays on lead mining, sheep farming and hand knitting, and craft exhibitions on drystone walling and butter making.

Traditional stone barns and drystone walls near Muker

5 MUKER

Distance: 1½ miles / 2.4 km

Map: OS Landranger 98 / OS Outdoor Leisure 30 GR: SD 911978

How to get there: Muker is high up in Swaledale, nine miles west of Reeth on the serpentine B6270, which is narrow in places. Sat nav: DL11 6QH.

Parking: Only limited parking is available in front of the pub, but there is a pay and display facility by the bridge.

Dwarfed by the imposing mass of Kisdon Hill and surrounded on all sides by lofty, poetically named fells, the hamlet of Muker lies in its valley like some sleeping beast. Beside the Straw Beck, whose bridge is one of the most romantic in the dale, this Norse settlement expanded in the days of lead mining. In breathtaking scenery, unspoilt and unchanged, the village is at the hub of a number of heroic walks to Lovely Seat, Great Shunner Fell, High Seat, Nine Standards Rigg and the wild land of crags and torrents around Keld to the north. There is no finer or more inspiring walking country in the whole of England.

This gentle saunter along the banks of the infant Swale gives you all the grandeur of the mountains without the exhaustion. An interesting feature of this walk is the large number of imposing, traditional stone barns, which inhabit many of the fields along the way.

THE PUB — THE FARMERS ARMS once slaked the thirsts of local miners. One of three former village alehouses, it is the only one to survive to modernity, and offers a warm welcome to walkers and cyclists in its cosy twin rooms. The menu includes popular Sunday roasts and locally brewed ale. A holiday apartment is available to rent opposite the pub.
www.farmersarmsmuker.co.uk ☎ 01748 886297.

The Walk

❶ Go left from the pub and left again by the church, swinging left and right to find a footpath sign 'To Keld'. Follow a track past the vicarage and continue, going uphill at the bend. Continue forward through the gates into a wood, and proceed in the same direction, going through further gates. Drop down right to a barn. Arc sharply right to the **Ramps Holme footbridge** and walk along the riverbank to a wicket gate.

❷ Go right through the gate, following the sign to **Muker** and walking along a distinctive flagged footway through a series of gated wall gaps. Head for the church tower, arcing right back into Muker.

The Farmers Arms

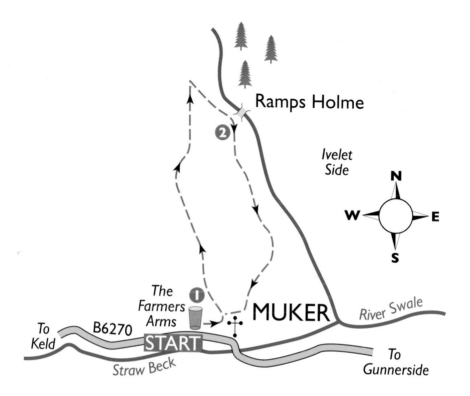

Places of interest nearby

St Mary the Virgin Church dates from 1580. Its most fascinating feature is its east window, with pastoral scenery representing the area around Muker: the Swale, the Straw Beck, Kisdon Hill and local fellside walls.

On the wall of the old school to the left of the pub are two fading memorial plaques to former pupils. **Richard Kearton** (1862–1928) was a naturalist, author and lecturer. His brother **Cherry Kearton** (1871–1940) was an explorer and wildlife photographer. Both men were highly regarded Attenborough-type pioneers of the day. Their former home in the nearby hamlet of Thwaite is now a popular hotel named in their honour.

Hardraw Force

6 HARDRAW

Distance: 3¼ miles / 5.2 km (including falls visit)

Map: OS Landranger 98 / OS Outdoor Leisure 30 GR: SD 867913

How to get there: Take the A684 north-west from Hawes for about 1½ miles, go through Appersett, cross New Bridge, and turn first right onto a minor road to reach the hamlet of Hardraw. Sat nav: DL8 3LZ.

Parking: Park in the inn car park or on the street.

The tiny settlement of Hardraw is situated at the foot of Abbotside Common in a sylvan spot overlooking Fossdale Gill; its epic geology has drawn visitors for centuries. Falling 100 feet in one plunge, Hardraw Force is one of the most spectacular waterfalls in the country. The beauty spot's reputation attracted the attention of the celebrated French tightrope walker Charles Blondin, who walked across the chasm whilst cooking an omelette! In more recent times, Hardraw welcomed Kevin Costner, who appeared in a famous scene at the foot of the falls in *Robin Hood: Prince of Thieves*.

Using a spooky old miners' track on a plateau at the edge of the moor, our stroll passes Yorkshire's very own Easter Island idols, strange families of cairns thrusting up like sea stacks with their stone siblings. Dropping down to a delightful dell path by the gill, this is a walk of contrasting sights, sounds and earthy smells.

THE PUB THE GREEN DRAGON INN dates from the 13th century and provides the warmest of welcomes with its beamed ceilings, flagged floors, inglenooks and its traditional snug. The inn serves wholesome, locally sourced food and a selection of Yorkshire ales; there are eight letting bedrooms and a campsite. www.greendragonhardraw. com ☎ 01969 667392.

The Green Dragon

The Walk

1 Turn left from the inn, and go immediately left, following the footpath sign to **Simonstone** through a gate, over a courtyard and up some steps. Continue forward into a field wallside on flagstones. Gradually veer away from the wall right, on a rising cobbled way in the direction of a copse and a house. Climb some steps and weave left to a stile. Cross left, and climb more steps into a second field; swing right at the side of the house to the signpost, and go through the gated wall gap to the right.

2 Go forward over a meadow on the flagged path, and go through a gated wall gap by a barn. Continue wallside in the next field, passing in front of **Simonstone Hall Hotel** and swinging right to a wall gap. Go through left, and turn right on the access drive, continuing to the lane.

3 Turn left on the lane, passing the back of the hotel, and continue for 150 metres. Turn right on the access drive to **Low Shaw**, climbing up and passing the bungalows; go left of the barns on the concrete hardstanding. Arc right at the back of the barns; then go left uphill fieldside to a gate.

4 Go through into a second field, heading towards a barn, and swing right to a gate. Continue through into a third field, steering left towards a copse and a wall corner (there is a large sycamore in the wall apex). Go left here, following the wall up to a stile. Cross and keep forward through the bracken, climbing up and right towards a clump of trees (the path is indeterminate at this point). Continue, forking right to the foot of the shales, and climb up to find a cairn and a plateau track.

5 Turn left on the level track, passing the successive lines of cairns, and follow the wall down towards the lane, dropping down left and going through a wall gap by a gate. Swing right on a green track, and drop down left through bracken to a ladder stile. Cross to the lane.

6 Turn right along the lane for 100 metres. Fork left, following a footpath sign to 'High Shaw ½ mile'. Walk to the right of the barn, turn briefly left, and then turn right over a ladder stile and left downhill wallside. Cross a stile in the field bottom, enter the edge of a wood by the gill, and cross a second stile, continuing for 100 metres.

To Thwaite

Shaw Gill

6

▲▲▲ *Cairns*

7

8

4

5

HARDRAW

9

■ *Low Shaw*

Hardraw Force

Simonstone Hall

The Green Dragon

3

2

To Sedbusk

1

To A684 & Hawes

START

River Ure

To Hawes

N
W — E
S

7 Go left over a stile into a field and follow the middle path, swinging right between the top two trees and over a stream. Go through a gated wall gap to a second field, continuing over the field to another gated wall gap. Go through to **High Shaw** and turn right, following the footpath sign between the outbuildings to a lane.

8 Turn sharp right, and walk for 150 metres. Turn left through a wall gap down a ladder to the gillside path, and go left, passing a number of cascades using the flagged path. Beguiled by the big drop, most tourists miss this wonderful spot. Look out here for kingfishers and rare ferns. Go through a gate by the bridge and keep left, swinging left to the lane.

9 Turn right along the lane for 200 metres to the **Low Shaw** access, and go right, following the footpath sign at the side of **Simonstone Hall** over a stile and through a gate; drop down to the right of a barn to the outward route. Retrace your steps back to the inn.
Entry to Hardraw Force is via the inn; a small fee is payable.

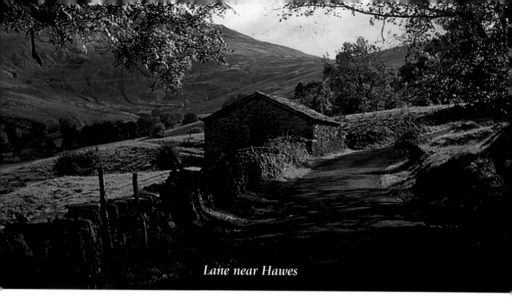

Lane near Hawes

7 Hawes

Distance: 2 miles / 3.2 km

Map: OS Landranger 98 / OS Outdoor Leisure 30 GR: SD 872899

How to get there: Make your way to the centre of Hawes, which is on the A684, at the head of Wensleydale. Sat nav: DL8 3RD.

Parking: Park on the street or in the pay and display car park off Gayle Lane, to the east of the town.

Encircled by grand fells, bustling Hawes takes its name from the word *hals*, meaning a pass between mountains. Formerly a rugged, agricultural place, filled with shops selling sheep dip, cattle medicines and milk pails, it is now a tourist haunt, with hosts of tea rooms, cafés and pubs, although the traditional industries of ropemaking and cheesemaking continue to flourish.

This short amble through meadows along part of the Pennine Way takes you to the picturesque sister settlement of Gayle, although there was no kindred love lost here. Until the First World War, for some reason lost in time, a simmering feud existed between the people of Hawes and Gayle, and there were many bare-knuckle fights. Now, the much-painted hamlet, with its pretty beck bridge and narrow alleys with quaint names like Marridales, Beckstones, Garris and Thundering Lane, is peace itself. Although poor, Gayle was the most famous centre in Wensleydale for the hand-knitting of gloves, caps and jerseys, the old cottage industry going back to the 16th century and surviving longer here than anywhere else. To save fuel, women and children would 'go a-sitting', gathering in each other's homes around a peat fire with their needles, telling ghost stories.

THE PUB THE BOARD INN is a welcoming, family-run inn. Centrally placed and popular with locals and tourists alike, it offers hearty, locally sourced fare and ales in its twin rooms. It has five letting bedrooms.
www.theboardinn.co.uk ☎ 01969 667223.

The Walk

1 Turn left from the inn along the street, and fork right to the church. Turn right into the churchyard, and go right by the entrance door, going through to a path. This large church, **St Margaret's**, was built in 1851 at a cost of £2,300. Turn left and go through a wall gap, forking right on a causeway and following a sign alongside the **Gayle Beck**. Go through a second wall gap, and swing right at the back of the creamery, going through two gates to the road. Turn left along the footway for 100 metres.

2 Turn right, following the **'Pennine Way'** sign at the side of the bus shelter, between the houses. Cross the back lane, keeping straight forward, and go through a wicket gate and then left over a field to a second wicket gate. Go through and cross a small field to a third wicket gate, going through to a lane.

3 Turn right on the lane, following the 'Pennine Way' sign, and follow the lane left, right and left uphill to a tall, small barn. Turn right along the lane to the junction.

4 Turn left at the junction, and walk on to the **Gaudy Lane** junction on the right; keep going forward for a further 40 metres.

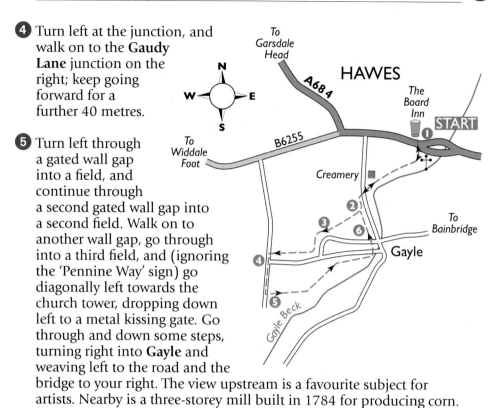

5 Turn left through a gated wall gap into a field, and continue through a second gated wall gap into a second field. Walk on to another wall gap, go through into a third field, and (ignoring the 'Pennine Way' sign) go diagonally left towards the church tower, dropping down left to a metal kissing gate. Go through and down some steps, turning right into **Gayle** and weaving left to the road and the bridge to your right. The view upstream is a favourite subject for artists. Nearby is a three-storey mill built in 1784 for producing corn.

6 Turn left and rejoin the outward route, retracing your steps back to Hawes and the inn.

Places of interest nearby

Apart from the many craft and gift shops, Hawes has a number of attractions. The **Dales Countryside Museum** (www.dalescountrysidemuseum.org.uk ☎ 01969 666210) is housed in a Victorian railway station. It tells the story of the Yorkshire Dales in an array of exhibits and regular events, the attractions including interactive displays, an outdoor trail and a café. Elsewhere, traditional ropemakers **Outhwaite's** (www.ropemakers.co.uk ☎ 01969 667487) demonstrate the ancient craft in an interesting visitor centre with free entry.

View of the town

8 ASKRIGG

Distance: 3 miles / 4.8 km

Map: OS Landranger 98 / OS Outdoor Leisure 30 GR: SD 948911

How to get there: Askrigg is north of the A684 near Bainbridge. Sat nav: DL8 3HQ.

Parking: Park on the street.

Askrigg is an attractive little town from every point of the compass: fells roll back from it and meadows creep up to it. It was once the centre of the local lead mining, knitting and clockmaking industries, more timepieces being produced here than anywhere else in the North Riding.

This stroll through fields to the hamlets of Newbiggin and Nappa Scar revels in some of the stirring history of the area.

THE PUB THE KING'S ARMS is an historic and atmospheric old inn built in 1760. This glorious example of the English pub, in all its warmth and quirkiness, was chosen as the setting for the 'Drovers Arms' in the hit TV series *All Creatures Great and Small*. A yawning inglenook fireplace, ancient beams and stone floors exude a robust and timeless charm. Examine the walls to find memorabilia of past visitors, and look up in the main bar to discover a collection of ceiling hooks where reins and saddles were hung by former landlord John Pratt, whose horse Imperatrix won the St Leger Stakes in 1782. The inn serves a highly regarded seasonal menu, with the emphasis on fresh local produce including fish and game from the nearby moors, together with a selection of Yorkshire ales. Adjacent accommodation is available. ☎ 01969 650113.

The King's Arms

The Walk

1 Turn left from the inn along the street, arcing left, and go left again on a lane signposted to **Muker**. Part-ascend the 1-in-4 hill, walking past **Hargill House** to the left, and go right opposite **Lee gate**, following a footpath sign through a gated wall gap.

2 Follow the wall down over a field, and swing left to a gap by a gate. Go through into a second field, veering left to a gap by a gate. Go through, continuing on a path between walls, swinging left and right over a beck into **Newbiggin**. It must have the tiniest village green in the country!

3 Go to the left of the green, between the cottages, and go through a gate, keeping wallside; walk over this first field and then cross five more fields in the same general direction using the gates and wall gaps. In the seventh field, veer left to a gated wall gap and go through into the eighth field, steering left to the field corner. Go through the gated wall gap into the ninth field, steering diagonally right to the wall corner and a barn and keeping the same general direction; cross the tenth and eleventh fields through gated wall gaps. Go through a wall gap in the twelfth field and turn right, following the wall down to the hamlet of **Nappa Scar**. Continue to the road and turn left.

4 Walk down the road for 200 metres and swing right downhill into **Nappa Hall** entrance.

5 Swing left and turn right on the tack passing the hall. This was bestowed on James Metcalfe by a gratefully victorious Henry V after the Battle of Agincourt in 1415 to acknowledge the provision of his subject's 100 archers. So prominent were the Metcalfes in the 16th century that 300 family members, all on white steeds, attended Sir Christopher Metcalfe when he was made High Sheriff of Yorkshire in 1556. Another resident of the hall – Sir Thomas Metcalfe, who was colourfully known as the 'Black Knight' – laid siege to Raydale House near Semerwater in 1671 after a feud with his neighbours. Several combatants were wounded and two were killed in the fracas, which is now regarded as the last act of domestic warfare in the country. Mary, Queen of Scots, was allowed to visit Nappa Hall whilst a prisoner at nearby Bolton Castle. Continue for 150 metres and go right through a gate following a footpath sign, going left across a field to a second gate. Go through and left over the next field towards a barn, climbing a stile and going through a gate on the right to the lane.

6 Turn right on **Low Gate** Lane, continuing uphill to the road.

7 Swing left at the junction into Askrigg. Go left again round the bend, and right back to the pub.

Places of interest nearby

St Oswald's Church, near the pub, is said to be the biggest and stateliest in the whole of Wensleydale. It has an interesting connection with this walk: the south chapel was founded in 1468 by James Metcalfe of Nappa Hall, the last of his direct descendants being buried here in 1756.

Aysgarth Falls

9 CARPERBY

Distance: 3½ miles / 5.6 km

Map: OS Landranger 98 / OS Outdoor Leisure 30 GR: SE 008899

How to get there: Carperby is best reached from the A684 in Aysgarth. Take the minor road north from the river for about ½ mile, and go right at the crossroads to arrive at the Wheatsheaf on your left. Sat nav: DL8 4DF.

Parking: Park at the inn or on the street.

Carperby's restrained prettiness reflects its sober past as a centre of Quakerism. At the foot of the steep fell, the Friends' Meeting House of 1864 stands proud amidst lines of cottages, some bearing 17th-century date marks on their lintels. On the green and around the prominent village cross, markets were once held, Carperby being credited with breeding the first Wensleydale sheep in 1838.

This stroll takes you over a mosaic of walled fields, whose boundaries have hardly changed in millennia, to the world-famous Aysgarth Falls. This spectacular and supremely picturesque succession of cataracts on the Ure has attracted numerous artists and photographers over the years; the set-to between Robin and Little John in *Robin Hood: Prince of Thieves* was also filmed here. Following the river through Freeholders' Wood, the route takes in the Upper, Middle and Lower Falls before returning on an old lane to Carperby.

Yorkshire Dales 30 Pub Walks

THE PUB THE WHEATSHEAF is an inn and former village butcher's shop dating from the 1800s. Now family-owned and tastefully upgraded, it provides thoroughly modern accommodation, two intimate bars and a restaurant serving wholesome Yorkshire fare and local ales. Famous previous guests have included the actress Greta Garbo, and the author James Herriot, who spent his honeymoon here. www.wheatsheafinwensleydale.co.uk ☎ 01969 663216.

The Wheatsheaf

The Walk

❶ Follow the **Aysgarth** footpath sign directly opposite the inn, going through a gate into a field. Go right through a second gate into a field and turn left, following a wall down for 100 metres to a signpost. Turn right to find a gate in the field corner and go through, walking over two fields using the wall gaps. Turn left wallside down a long, narrow third field to a wall gap. Go through onto **Low Lane** and turn right to the road.

❷ Go left, using the verge for 50 metres, and fork right through a wall gap following the sign to Aysgarth. Walk parallel to the road over the first field; go through a wall gap into a second field, veering away from the road to the right, and keep to the right of the metal-fenced copse to find a stile. Cross into a third field, heading towards the wood, and negotiate the gated stile. Enter the wood, and drop down to a kissing gate. Go through, keeping right, and drop down left to a second kissing gate. Go through and drop down some steps to the car park. Turn right, following the sign to the **Upper Falls** along the path to the bridge. (This was originally erected in 1539 as a crossing for packhorses.) Veer right along the riverbank to the falls, and return to the car park.

❸ Follow the footpath sign forward to the **Lower Falls**, crossing over the car park to the left of the visitor centre, and take the signed footpath to the **Middle and Lower Falls**, crossing the road to the right and going left into **Freeholders' Wood**. Renowned for its hazelnuts, this is the only remaining fragment of the ancient Forest of Wensleydale of any size. Follow the well-defined path, visit the Middle Falls to the right, and return to the path; go through a gate to view the Lower Falls before returning to the path again.

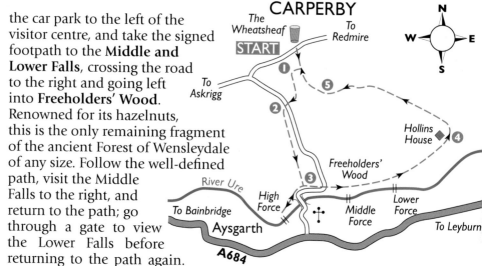

Go through a gate and keep forward on the path, swinging right to a further gate. Go through, and continue to a stile and the signpost marked 'FP Castle Bolton'. Go left over the stile into a field and swing right, following the fence down to the gated wall gap and a sign marked 'Redmire and Castle Bolton'. Go through and continue over a field to the barns at **Hollins House**, going through a gate and swinging right on the farm access road.

4 Swing left on the track, ignoring the footpath sign to the right, and keep left over the cattle grid and the route of the abandoned railway, going through a gate to **Low Lane**. Walk on about 200 metres past the farmhouse on the left to the signpost marked '**Carperby Village**'.

5 Turn right through a gated wall gap into a field, steering left through the wall gap over the next field to the outward signpost; retrace your steps back to the inn.

Places of interest nearby

Once a water-powered cotton mill, the nearby **Yorkshire Carriage Museum** at Yore Mill (☎ 01969 663399) exhibits 50 antique horse-drawn vehicles, including coaches, fire engines and hansom cabs, together with coaching ephemera.

Bolton Castle

10 REDMIRE

Distance: 2¼ miles / 3.6 km

Map: OS Landranger 98 / OS Outdoor Leisure 30 GR: SE 045913

How to get there: Redmire lies west of Leyburn. The best access is from the A684, turning off in Wensley village to head north-west on an unnamed road for about four miles. Sat nav: DL8 4EA.

Parking: Parking is limited outside the inn. There is alternative parking on Hargill Lane (north of the inn) near the railway bridge.

With crow's-nest views, Redmire looks serenely out on Wensleydale, its cottages, ancient green and church sitting snugly under the gaze of a towering sentinel to the rear. A former lead mining settlement whose name derives from the reedy lake that once occupied the low land at the south of the village, Redmire is dominated by Bolton Castle, a remarkable, largely preserved fortress which has been described as a climax of English military architecture. Misbehave in the medieval precincts and you might imagine a crossbow bolt zinging past your ear!

This walk takes you over tracks that might well have been trodden by Mary, Queen of Scots, who was incarcerated in the castle in 1568. The walk passes alongside the track of an old railway line and through fields to the village of Castle Bolton.

THE PUB THE BOLTON ARMS is a cherubic little inn with an inviting lounge and a small dining room. Dating from the 17th century, it was originally a farmhouse, but in recent centuries it has been the centre of village life. Locals and visitors mingle in its attractive bar to chat and savour its beguiling atmosphere, wholesome menu and Yorkshire ales. The inn has five letting bedrooms. www.boltonarmsredmire. co.uk ☎ 01969 624336.

The Walk

1 Turn left from the inn along **Hargill Lane**, and walk on uphill towards the railway bridge. Go under the bridge and turn immediately left, following the footpath sign.

2 Cross the footbridge over the **Apedale Beck**, and continue walking parallel to the embankment. Swing right across a footbridge over a ditch, arcing away from the embankment over a field and heading to the left of a barn. In the field corner, go through a gated wall gap and steer left over the next field, heading towards **Bolton Castle**. Go through a second wall gap, and proceed over the field bottom towards the castle, negotiating a third wall gap; then turn sharp right, following the line of a wall towards a gate. Go through the wall gap to the right of the gate, and continue on the track, turning left into Bolton Castle. This is undoubtedly one of the finest castles in Europe, so you should allow plenty of time for visiting the fortress and its grounds. Construction was begun in 1379 by Sir Richard Scrope, Lord Chancellor of England at the time of Richard II. The fortress has a wealth of chambers and rooms to explore: dark corridors, spiral staircases and cobbled courtyards add to the mystery and excitement that culminates, for many, in a visit to Mary, Queen of Scots', bedchamber. The current occupant of the castle, despite its overwhelmingly martial presence, has created a relaxing family home.

3 Having explored the castle, turn right downhill and walk south along the quiet lane, going left on the bend to follow the footpath sign over a stile, and continuing between drystone walls. Swing left and go through a gate, keeping left over the long field to arrive at the third of the previously negotiated wall gaps. Go through to the right, and make your way back to the embankment.

4 Cross the embankment, forking right; go through a gap in a fence and cross a field leftward, using the stepping stones over the boggy ground to find a gate. Go through and forward to a stile. Cross, and go immediately left through a wall gap, following the wall down to a fence. Go through the gap, and cross the **Apedale Beck** on the stepping stones. Go through a wall gap, and cross a meadow to another wall gap, going through and weaving leftward over a field at the back of the cottages. Swing right to a stile and cross, continuing on a track to **Hargill Lane**.

5 Turn right down the lane, and walk back to the inn.

Places of interest nearby

The attractions at **Bolton Castle** (www.boltoncastle.co.uk ☎ 01969 623981) include costumed guided tours, archery demonstrations and falconry displays. The castle has a shop, a tea room, a wild boar park and a garden.

Looking towards Penhill from Wensley

11 WENSLEY

Distance: 5½ miles / 8.9 km

Map: OS Landranger 99 / OS Outdoor Leisure 30 GR: SE 093898

How to get there: Wensley is on the A684, just over a mile south-west of the market town of Leyburn. Sat nav: DL8 4HJ.

Parking: Park in the inn car park or in the parking area near the church.

Wensley village gives its name to the whole glorious dale, and there are more evocative descriptions of Wensleydale's views – waterfalls, castles, abbeys and pretty hamlets – than you can throw a thesaurus at. Wensley itself, an estate village tied to Bolton Hall, lies on the banks of the beautiful River Ure. It consists of little more than a few cottages, a church and a wonderful little pub.

This epic walk takes you over pastures and through the market town of Leyburn to the soaring limestone scar of Leyburn Shawl. The return route is over meadows and through the fields of Wensley Park.

THE PUB THE THREE HORSESHOES is a traditional whitewashed Dales inn that surveys the wonderful valley of the Ure from its sunny terrace. A roadside favourite of cyclists and walkers, it offers a cosy two-roomed interior and serves hearty homemade food and local ales. Flower-smothered in summer, and with a wood burner and an open fire for the colder months, it is a popular refreshment point in all seasons. www.thethreehorseshoeswensley.co.uk ☎ 01969 622327.

The Walk

❶ Go left from the inn, downhill towards the church. Dating from 1245, **Holy Trinity Church** is full of ancient treasures: a famous Flemish brass, many armorial shields and a fine Bolton pew. Turn left on **Low Lane**, and go left again after 150 metres, following the arrow marker past **Glebe Cottage**. Swing right uphill, and just before **Rectory Garth**, go through the second gate on the right, following the arrow marker left across a small field. Cross a stile, veering right across the second field, and drop down in the field bottom towards a power line post. Keep going forward to a stile, crossing into a third field. Stay fenceside to the corner, and go left uphill at the edge of a copse. Go right over a stile, following the arrow marker, and go right over another stile into **Leyburn Old Glebe Nature Reserve**; then keep left wallside. Keep going in the same general direction, crossing ten more fields using stiles and wall gaps, until you come to a barn.

❷ A few yards on, turn left, following an arrow marker over a stile, and keep fieldside to the corner. Go right across a stile, and continue along the long meadow, going to the right of the ash tree in the corner; cross two ladder stiles to the railway line. Cross, and weave right and left to a third ladder stile. Cross, and go right over a field to a gap in the wall; cross into the second field, and go right to the road. Turn right on the footway into **Leyburn**.

❸ In Leyburn, walk towards the **Bolton Arms**, going to the right of it and down **Commercial Square**. Weave right, left and right, following the sign, and go through two gates to the **Shawl**. Proceed straight forward through a series of wall gaps and over three fields, continuing on a woodland path and following the ridge path as it swings right. Keep wallside, following the arrow marker, and enter the wood, continuing on the well-defined path for about ½ mile. Drop down left to a stile. Cross leftward over a field, and at the second stile, fork right to the smallest of the hawthorn trees. Cross a third stile, keeping the same general direction, and then a fourth stile, heading down the long field and bearing left to the corner.

4 Go left on the track, following the yellow arrow marker through a gate. Pass the farm buildings to the left, and drop down left, right and left again to the road. Cross and go through a gate, following a footpath sign over a small field. Cross a stile to the railway line.

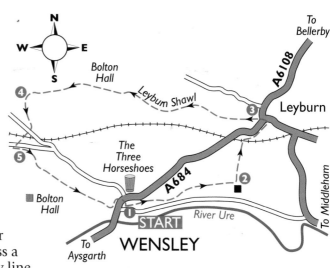

Cross over the line. Go through a gate, following the arrow marker, and steer right across a field. Go through a further gate to the lane.

5 Turn left for 250 metres; then go right, following a footpath sign into a wood. Turn left after 50 metres to follow a track bearing right and left fieldside. Go left at the 'PRIVATE' sign, and walk on in an arc to the right to enter a large field, walking in the direction of a big central oak tree. Weave left and right to the Bolton Hall access road. Continue through Wensley Park to the A684, and go left back to the inn.

Places of interest nearby

Bolton Castle is five miles north-west of Wensley (see Walk 10).

Just across the valley from Wensley is the ruined but evocative **Middleham Castle** (www.english-heritage.org.uk/visit/places/middleham-castle ☎ 01969 623899), the childhood home of Richard III. Begun in 1190, it became known as the 'Windsor of the North'. Exhibits include a replica of the Middleham Jewel, discovered by metal detector users on a bridleway near the castle in 1985. The original was acquired by the Yorkshire Museum in York for £2.5 million.

Beyond Middleham, along the A6108, is **Brymor Dairy** (www.brymordairy.co.uk ☎ 01677 460337), which has an ice cream parlour and café serving over 35 different flavours of ice cream and sorbet.

Falls on the Walden Beck

12 WEST BURTON

Distance: 1½ miles / 2.4 km

Map: OS Landranger 98 / OS Outdoor Leisure 30 **GR:** SE 018867

How to get there: West Burton lies south of the A684 Leyburn–Hawes road. Take the B6160 east of Aysgarth and then a minor road. **Sat nav:** DL8 4JY.

Parking: Park around the spacious green.

Set in a necklace of sweet fells, West Burton has been described as the best village in the whole of Wensleydale. Its spacious green – the sixth biggest in England – and its attractive waterfalls on the Walden Beck give it great charm. At the junction of Bishopdale and Waldendale, and surrounded by the turret heights of Penhill, Naughtberry Hill and the mighty Addleborough, it was once an important market town. Today it earns a living from agriculture and tourism, its tranquillity protected by twin no through roads.

In scenes of reckless beauty, the walk's elevated pastures give you just a peep of Waldendale. You'll skirt the foot of Walden Moor, whose crest is marked by the site of an ancient settlement and field system, before descending to Walden Beck waterfall.

The Fox and Hounds overlooking the village green

THE PUB THE FOX AND HOUNDS overlooks the green and is as hospitable as a cottage parlour, providing a rustic yet eclectic menu including steaks from the village butcher and pizzas from its own oven. Every morsel is made on the premises. The inn has a well-stocked bar serving local brews, a cosy dining room and a traditional stone cottage at the rear providing overnight accommodation. www.foxandhoundswestburton.co.uk ☎ 01969 663111.

The Walk

❶ Go right from the pub, and pass the school and **West Burton House**, continuing on a track towards a farm.

❷ Go left on a stony track before the farm, then swing left, right and left again to a quiet lane.

❸ Turn right along the lane for 200 metres, then go left through a gated wall gap, following the footpath sign to '**Cote Bridge ½ mile**'. In the field, keep to the right of an electricity pole, dropping down on the bank, and go left at the footpath sign over a footbridge spanning the **Walden Beck**.

4 Turn diagonally left over a meadow, following the footpath sign to **Riddings**, and cross a ladder stile over a wall, continuing over a field and through a gate and keeping left for 150 metres. Go left through the gated wall gap. Steer right over a field, go through a gated wall gap, and continue past Riddings to the next gated wall gap. Continue over two more fields and gated wall gaps; in the third field, ignore the track downhill to the left, instead forking right to find a gated wall gap. Go through and drop down to the footpath sign.

5 Follow the footpath sign and the wall to the left, and go through the gated wall gap to the left of the barn, dropping down left through the gate and down some steps to the falls. Swing right and left over the bridge, going right by the cottages and then left back into West Burton.

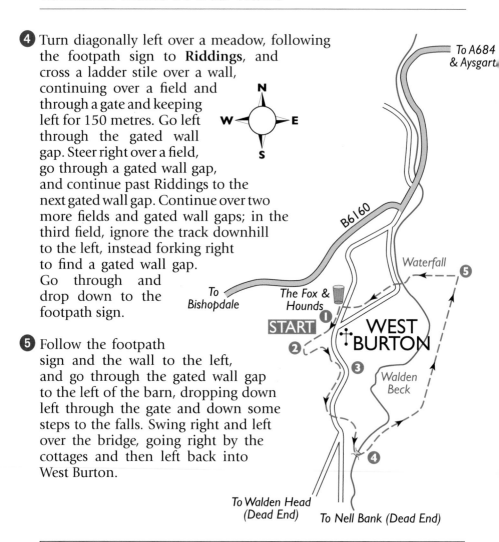

Places of interest nearby

In West Burton is the family run **Cat Pottery** (www.catpottery. co.uk ☎ 01969 663273), a thriving business since 1982. It produces ceramic, metallic and granite cats.
In the nearby village of Aysgarth are the famous **Aysgarth Falls** and the **Yorkshire Carriage Museum** (see Walk 9).

The River Cover

13 CARLTON-IN-COVERDALE

Distance: 2 miles / 3.2 km

Map: OS Landranger 99 / OS Outdoor Leisure 30 GR: SE 067847

How to get there: Carlton, one of a number of similarly named villages in Yorkshire, is in Coverdale, its valley linking Wensleydale with Wharfedale. Sat nav: DL8 4BB.

Parking: Park outside the inn.

With the remains of the old abbey at Coverham and evocative reminders of the days of coaches, packhorses and lead mining, Coverdale sleeps on, unmolested by traffic, its broad canvas of pastures and wide fells guarded by the imposing heights of Dead Man's Hill and Great Whernside. Amazingly, though, the road up the valley was the coach route from London to Richmond. In the centre of the dale, Carlton once presided over the 'courts of the forest', and it is thought that an ancient parliament was held there to settle disputes. According to the Middleham accounts of 1465–7, Carlton had a common oven, a corn mill and a brewery.

Circling the river, this stroll takes you through fields towards the village of West Scrafton, where the writer James Herriot spent many holidays.

The Foresters Arms

THE PUB THE FORESTERS ARMS dates from the 17th century and is a classic English hostelry. With ancient oak beams and open fires, it blazes a welcome; its rescue from extinction in 2011 by the local community adds extra purpose to a visit to this special place. Serving locally produced food and ales, it has three letting bedrooms and a lively social calendar. Having survived the lean years of isolation and lack of custom, it now thrives, with ramblers, cyclists and seekers of solitude visiting in increasing numbers.
www.forestersarms-carlton.co.uk ☎ 01969 640272.

The Walk

1 Go left from the inn along the road for 250 metres. Turn left, following the footpath sign to **Flats Hill** and steering left to the gated wall gap. Go through and continue forward over six fields, using the wall gaps, to arrive at the lane.

2 Turn immediately left, going through a gate following the sign to **Cover Lane**. Cross a field and head for a middle wall, crossing to the left of the gate. Cross and continue to the right of a barn; go through the gated wall gap, following the wall down to the 'FP Carlton' sign, and go through a wall gap to the lane.

3 Turn left down the lane, walk round the bend, and cross the **River Cover** on **Nathwaite Bridge**, climbing uphill for 300 metres. The Cover is a delectable and boisterous mountain stream that rushes from its watershed between **Buckden Pike** and **Great Whernside**. It holds good heads of trout and grayling, and although shallow and difficult to fish, it is the delight of anglers.

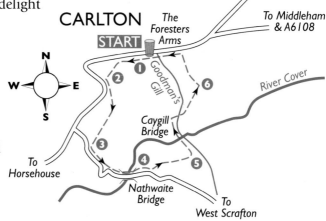

4 Turn left, following the footpath sign 'FP West Scrafton'. Do not continue straight forward here: enter the field, but go immediately right through a gate into another field, and then steer right away from the **Cover Valley** towards a fragment of a wall. Go through and continue fenceside, veering right and left to the footpath sign on top of the mound; fork left, following the sign to **Caygill Bridge**.

5 Head downhill towards the trees, weave left, and go through a gate, continuing fenceside beside the gill. Swing left to Caygill Bridge. Cross, and bear right across the second smaller footbridge; go through a gate, swinging right and left around the base of the mini hill and following the footpath sign uphill. Follow the line of the hawthorns, and then veer right across a field, following the line of a wall down towards a barn. Go through a gate to the left.

6 Walk down a track between two walls, continuing between the cottages to the road. Turn left back to the inn.

Places of interest nearby

Back along the Coverham road, in the Tupgill Park estate, is the remarkable **Forbidden Corner** (www.theforbiddencorner.co.uk ☎ 01969 640638), self-dubbed 'The Strangest Place in the World'. Its eccentric and bizarre collection of strange statues and follies combine the creepiness of the ghost train with the puzzlement of the maze. Pre-booking essential.

A farmhouse in Bishopdale

(courtesy of B. Meadows)

14 THORALBY

Distance: 4½ miles / 7.2 km

Map: OS Landranger 98 / OS Outdoor Leisure 30 GR: SD 999868

How to get there: Thoralby is best reached from the B6160 – the only road up Bishopdale – by coming off the A684 just east of Aysgarth. Sat nav: DL8 3SU.

Parking: Park in the small car park in front of the inn or on the lane.

Bishopdale's contours are closely compressed between the heights of Naughtberry Hill and Stake Fell: in just five miles, the lonely valley of the Bishopdale Beck falls nearly 900 feet to Thoralby. A retiring village, its name meaning 'Thorold's farm', it is set under the hill on the 'sunny side of the valley'. The settlement of Newbiggin on the opposite slope is said to be 'on the money side'. Thoralby has been spruced up in recent years, some of its neat old cottages providing accommodation for the few fortunate tourists.

This reasonably taxing but rewarding walk, some of it over rough ground, follows a steadily climbing track to the grouse butts on Heck Brow. With panoramic views of nearly half of Wensleydale, it descends on a parallel route back to Thoralby. This is not an outing for the gregarious. Normally only the lone Pacific mariner experiences this much solitude.

THE PUB

THE GEORGE INN is a dapper, delightful and homely little inn set before a cobbled courtyard and with beautiful rearward views of the surrounding dale. Built in 1732, it retains its yawning fireplace for cosy nights by the blaze and supplies everything but your fireside slippers. Its traditional hearty fare and local ales have been widely recommended. In recent years, it has added accommodation to its attractions, providing two letting bedrooms. www.thegeorgeinnthoralby.com ☎ 01969 663256.

The Walk

1 Turn right from the inn onto the lane for 300 metres, and go right at the signpost marked 'Busk Lane 4 Aysgarth 1¼'. Climb steeply up the track, going right and left. Walk on, passing **Swinacote Gill** to your left, and swing right and left, crossing **Hacker Gill Beck**. Keep climbing, and go through a gate, continuing onto the moorland and following a green track. Go through a second gate, and follow the wall down, swinging right and left to walk up and to the left of **Gayle Ing** – the prominent copse and farmhouse to your right. Go through a third gate, and continue up to the rise, walking on and swinging right for a further 250 metres. There are few reference points here, but the grouse butts to the left over the wall – accessed by a paving slab stile – should help to fix your position. Simply but effectively made from rough timber and tufts of ling, the grouse butts themselves melt

The George

into the landscape. Overall, this outward stretch of the walk is about 2¼ miles.

2 Turn sharp left through the tussock grass on a faint path running parallel to the drystone wall. Cross the line of a broken wall,

The map shows a walking route around Thoralby and Bishopdale, with labels including N/W/E/S compass, START, The George, To Aysgarth, THORALBY, Gayle Ing, Grouse Butts, BISHOPDALE, Bishopdale Beck, B6160, To A684 & Aysgarth, To Buckden.

following the path towards the wall corner, and swing right at the corner, continuing on a line parallel to the wall. Gradually veer away left from the wall and the beck, heading back down the **Bishopdale Valley**. Veer right to a gate, go through, and steer right at the edge of some tussock grass, dropping downhill and merging with a broken wall. Walk to the bridleway sign, and continue wallside; go through a gate to the second direction sign. Go right, following the bridleway, and left over a stream bed, forking right to a third sign and arcing left following the track marked 'PW Thoralby'. Go through a series of gates, and take the left fork, keeping the gill to your right; continue on the lane passing **Old Hall** (date stone 1641) back to the inn.

Places of interest nearby

At the west end of the village is a house marked with the initials 'MS' and with a date stone of 1704. Local legend says that treasure is buried here. An old man once dreamt that he saw a black teapot stuffed with gold sovereigns under the floor. From time to time, flagstones have been removed in an – as yet – futile search. If ramblers find any coins, they are asked to present them at the bar of the George Inn, where they will be rewarded with a free pint.

(courtesy of B. Meadows)

Dent Head Viaduct

15 DENT

Distance: 2 miles / 3.2 km

Map: OS Landranger 98 / OS Outdoor Leisure 2 GR: SD 705870

How to get there: The village of Dent is reached by narrow and winding roads either from the A684 at Sedbergh to the north-west or from the B6255 at Gayle Moor to the south-east. Sat nav: LA10 5QL.

Parking: Park in the inn car park or in the large pay and display facility north-west of the church.

Shoehorned into the serpentine valley of the Dee, Dent is perched high in the Yorkshire Dales National Park, although, paradoxically, the village has been annexed by Cumbria. Motoring here can be an epic and doubtful adventure: as your vehicle bounces over chariot-wide cobbled streets, you may wonder if, like Brigadoon, the place has been asleep for years. But such somnolence and isolation – Dent's own railway station is a perverse four miles away – has nurtured a proud independence down the years, the village once being one of the most important centres for hand-knitting. Dent has another claim to fame: Adam Sedgwick, the famous geologist, was born here in 1785. This

Cambridge Professor of Geology is commemorated by an inscribed pink granite monolith in the main street.

With long-distance fell views, this relaxing and uncomplicated walk takes you along the banks of the River Dee, returning over water meadows to Dent.

The village of Dent

THE PUB THE SUN INN has slaked local thirsts for over 300 years, and it continues to radiate the warmth and hospitality that hallmarks the English inn as one of the most unique and cherished social institutions in the world. It offers ancient beams, cheery open fires, locally brewed ales and wholesome food. There is also excellent bed and breakfast accommodation, and walkers, dogs and muddy boots are all welcome.
www.suninndent.co.uk ☎ 01539 625208.

The Walk

1 Turn left from the inn over the cobbled alley for 30 metres, and go right past **Church Gate Cottage** into the church grounds, dropping down some steps to the right of the church. Originally Norman, St Andrew's was last restored in 1889. Leave the churchyard, and go left on the road, dropping down to the **Dee Bridge**.

2 Go right over a stile, following a path signed to '**Middle Bridge**' over a field, and then turn left through a gate over a stream by the barn, crossing a stile and continuing on a raised footpath between two fields wallside. Follow the banks of the **Dee** upstream to the right, and cross a series of stiles to the footbridge.

To Sedbergh & A684

DENT

START

The Sun

River Dee

Footbridge

To B6255 & Ribblehead

Double Croft

To Kingsdale & Ingleton

N
W E
S

3 Turn right on what appears at first to be the dry bed of a stream, following this sunken path and continuing to a gate. Go through and swing right on **Double Croft Lane**.

4 Swing left past **Double Croft**, and go through a gate; swing right to a further gate. Go through and follow the hedge line down, arcing left and following a stream bank at the side of the meadow. Cross a ditch using a stile and a planked bridge, going left and right towards the neck of a narrow field. Go through a wall gap, and keep along the beck bank, going through a gated wall gap and then left over a bridge and through the gate to regain the outward path. Retrace your steps back to the inn.

Places of interest nearby

The fascinating exhibits in the **Dent Village Museum & Heritage Centre** (www.museumsintheyorkshiredales.co.uk ☎ 01539 625800) highlight the lives and social customs of former residents.

The access road from the south-east passes two dramatic viaducts on the **Settle–Carlisle Railway** (www.settle-carlisle.co.uk): Dent Head and Artengill. If you take the train from Settle or Ribblehead, you can appreciate these marvellous structures in style, alighting at Dent Station and then getting a taxi to the village.

Ribblehead Viaduct

16 RIBBLEHEAD

Distance: 2½ miles / 4 km

Map: OS Landranger 98 / OS Outdoor Leisure 2 GR: SD 764792

How to get there: The Station Inn is at Ribblehead near the railway station and the B6255/B6479 junction. Sat nav: LA6 3AS.

Parking: Park outside the inn or on the extensive grass verges near the junction.

Seared into the map with the force of a branding iron by the railway pioneers who created the Settle–Carlisle line, Ribblehead is best known for its amazing viaduct. Consisting otherwise of scattered farmhouses, the railway station and an inn, the hamlet is located slap-bang in the middle of Three Peaks country, named for the famous summits of Penyghent, Whernside and Ingleborough.

This stroll takes you first to the 24-arch marvel that is the Ribblehead Viaduct. Completed in 1871 at the cost of many lives, it is the centrepiece of the Settle–Carlisle Railway, which penetrates some of the most magnificent scenery in England. The 72 miles of track cost £47,500 per mile – an astronomical sum of money in the 1870s. The costliest stretch of all was the Ribblehead to Eden Vale section; Blea Moor Tunnel, beyond Ribblehead, averaged £45 per metre.

At the foot of Whernside, you'll wander towards Blea Moor signal box, passing under the line and returning via Batty Green, a location that was once home to the viaduct construction site. Deserted now, this wilderness then attracted men and women from every part of the kingdom. Nowadays, you can stand at leisure and glory in the views; the navvies, many of whom gave their lives to this place, are gone. Many are buried in local churchyards.

THE PUB THE STATION INN is stoutly built, with a cosy bar and dining room and adjacent bunkhouse accommodation. It's not the most sophisticated watering hole in Yorkshire, but as one recent walker observed, 'We were there for the location, not the wallpaper.' Another tramper noted, 'Nobody batted an eyelid at our soggy boots and dog,' a companion adding, 'The barmaid gave us towels to dry ourselves off and a timetable for the train times to Carlisle.' www.stationinnribblehead.co.uk ☎ 01524 241274.

The Station Inn

The Walk

1 Turn left from the inn along the road for 100 metres. Go left, following the bridleway sign on a pathway, and swing left under the viaduct on the broad track. Some of the viaduct pier foundations are 25 feet deep; the viaduct length is 1,320 feet. Swing right and left, going through a gate, and go right to the barns near **Gunnerfleet Farm**. Go through a second gate, cross the bridge over the **Winterscales Beck**, and turn right.

2 Follow the beck using the track, and swing left by a hillock to a gate. Go through, and continue to the track junction.

3 Turn right, following the sign to '**Deepdale 5½**' on a path crossing a stile by a cattle grid. Continue on a lane; just beyond **Winterscales**

Farm, go right, following the 'FP **Whernside'** sign over a humped-backed bridge on a rough track. Go through a gate, and head left towards the signal box. Swing right to the tunnel, and go through, under the railway line.

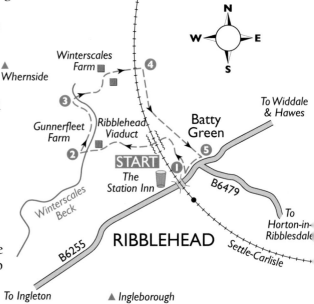

④ Turn right, walking alongside the railway line on a broad track, and continue to a stile, crossing and dropping down some steps to the left of the viaduct. Keep left over Batty Green to arrive at the road.

⑤ Turn right along the road, and walk back to the inn.

Places of interest nearby

In constructing the Settle–Carlisle line, hundreds of workers and their families – among them a large contingent of navvies from Ireland – died from accidents, injuries, overwork, malnutrition, smallpox and cholera. You can see a memorial to the victims down the road from Ribblehead in the cemetery of **Chapel-le-Dale Church**.

Hubberholme

(courtesy of B. Meadows)

17 HUBBERHOLME

Distance: 3½ miles / 5.6 km

Map: OS Landranger 98 / OS Outdoor Leisure 30 GR: SD 927783

How to get there: The best access to the tiny Upper Wharfedale village of Hubberholme is along the B6160, which runs between Grassington and the A684 near Aysgarth. Turn off westwards between Buckden and Cray. Sat nav: BD23 5JE.

Parking: Park in the inn car park.

The name Langstrothdale will linger long in the memory after a visit to this hidden valley of the Wharfe – a blithesome river – which is unspoilt, unsullied and totally unforgettable. In 1933, the novelist and playwright J. B. Priestley came here. Hubberholme has changed little since his car chugged up the dale, and the inn where he stopped for lunch is still here!

In a deeply carved valley, the hamlet consists of little more than the inn, a scattering of farmsteads, several old cottages and the beautifully sited church of St Michael. Wild flower meadows and ancient woodland clothe the valley sides, which rise abruptly to the sky.

This walk ascends the hill to the evocative Scar House. In 1652, George Fox, the founder of the Quakers, converted its owner, who established a Friends' Meeting House here. Through woodland, the path leads to Yockenthwaite – in old Norse, 'Eogan's clearing' – returning alongside the river accompanied by a Yorkshire mascot: the dipper.

THE PUB THE GEORGE INN is set in a nook by the Gill Beck. A whitewashed cocoon, it has thick walls, mullioned windows, flagstone floors and splendid fireplaces. Built in the 17th century as a farmhouse, it was once a vicarage, the caring clergyman placing a lighted candle in a window to signal to his parishioners that he was at home for blessings and succour. This lovely tradition continues whenever the inn is open. This beguiling place serves 'probably the best Sunday roast in Yorkshire' (*Yorkshire Post Magazine*) and local ales; it was awarded silver and bronze accolades in the 2017 British Pie Awards. The inn has four letting bedrooms. www.thegeorge-inn.co.uk ☎ 01756 760223.

The George Inn

The Walk

1 Cross the bridge from the inn, and swing right of the church, going left through a gate following a sign to **Yockenthwaite**. Take the right fork, signposted to **Scar House**, uphill. Climb the winding track, and cross the ladder stile by the National Trust sign; weave up right to Scar House, dated 1698. To the side of the house, which is now a National Trust holiday cottage, there is a small enclosure dotted with five trees. This is a former burial ground, although there are no headstones.

2 Walk to the left of the house, looking out for the yellow arrow marker on the side of a barn, and go right, following this marker at the back of the house; swing left to the signpost, and continue for 100 metres to the 'FP Yockenthwaite' sign. Turn left here through a gated wall gap, and weave left to the top of the tree line, following the path right to enter a wood through a wicket gate. Cross a rustic bridge, dropping down left, and continue on the track through two wall gaps. Keep going forward on the well-defined path, crossing three broken walls; then go through a wall gap, a gate and a further broken wall, continuing beyond the barn. Go left, following a footpath downhill and heading towards a bridge in the bottom. Follow the footpath sign right on a narrow track, and go through a wicket gate; then continue, going through a gate and leftward on a track downhill towards Yockenthwaite and a footpath sign. At the farmhouse, go left, following the 'Hubberholme' sign. A few hundred metres further upstream to your right, on the public footpath, is an ancient stone circle.

3 Swing right to the lower gate and the 'FP Hubberholme' sign, and go left through this and two more gates, swinging right to a wall gap. Go through and down some steps, and follow the footpath sign left along the riverbank. Continue on the well-defined footpath over a succession of gated and stiled fields back to Hubberholme, and turn right back to the inn.

Places of interest nearby

Visit the magical, Norman **St Michael's Church**: 'very rough interior', notes the Pevsner guidebook. Inside is an inscription to J. B. Priestley, whose ashes were scattered nearby: 'He loved the Dales and found Hubberholme one of the smallest and pleasantest places in the world.'

Kettlewell

(courtesy of B. Meadows)

18 KETTLEWELL

Distance: 4 miles / 6.4 km

Map: OS Landranger 98 / OS Outdoor Leisure 30 GR: SD 968723

How to get there: Kettlewell is north of Grassington on the B6160. Sat nav: BD23 5QZ.

Parking: Park in the inn car park or near the river bridge (fee payable).

Kettlewell is a rugged and beautiful place, and a sort of Heathrow for walkers and cyclists, with tracks, paths and the Yorkshire Dales Cycleway whizzing off in every direction. The airport allusion is apt: the surrounding hills of Great Whernside, Buckden Pike and my favourite, Old Cote Moor Top, rise to dizzy heights.

This is a leisurely river walk along the valley bottom to the hamlet of Starbotton and back. The only sounds you will hear on this ramble are the gurgling of the Wharfe, the splash of rising trout and the distant bubbling call of curlews.

The Wharfe valley between Kettlewell and Starbotton

THE PUB THE RACEHORSES HOTEL is a thoroughly modern hotel with ancient charms, its tranquil position between the Cam Beck and the River Wharfe proving irresistible to passing customers. A former 18th-century coaching inn, it offers 13 en-suite bedrooms, two bars and twin dining rooms with open fires for the winter months. The menu, using local ingredients, is extensive, Sunday lunches being particularly popular with walkers. www.racehorseshotel.co.uk ☎ 01756 760233.

The Walk

1 From the hotel, fork left on the lane, passing the village hall; walk up to the 'FP Starbotton' sign, and follow the sign uphill, climbing to a wicket gate. Go through, and after 20 metres, go left, following the well-defined path for about 1¾ miles above the valley, running

The Racehorses Hotel

parallel to the river. At the footpath sign, go left, and follow the additional signposts through a succession of gates into **Starbotton**.

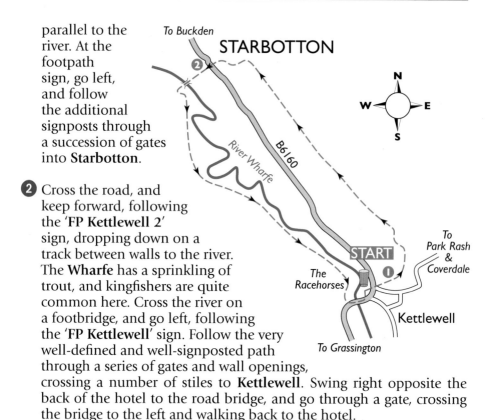

2 Cross the road, and keep forward, following the 'FP Kettlewell 2' sign, dropping down on a track between walls to the river. The **Wharfe** has a sprinkling of trout, and kingfishers are quite common here. Cross the river on a footbridge, and go left, following the 'FP Kettlewell' sign. Follow the very well-defined and well-signposted path through a series of gates and wall openings, crossing a number of stiles to **Kettlewell**. Swing right opposite the back of the hotel to the road bridge, and go through a gate, crossing the bridge to the left and walking back to the hotel.

Places of interest nearby

Just south of Kettlewell, along the B6160, is the famous rocky overhang known as **Kilnsey Crag**.

A few hundred yards from here is the award-winning and spectacularly situated **Kilnsey Park Estate** (www.kilnseypark. co.uk ☎ 01756 752150). This family attraction offers fly fishing on its trout farm, small animal enclosures, cycle hire and pony trekking. Its café and delicatessen specialise in Dales produce. Open every day.

The valley of Littondale

19 LITTON

Distance: 2¼ miles / 3.6 km

Map: OS Landranger 98 / OS Outdoor Leisure 30 **GR:** SD 908741

How to get there: Litton is around ten miles north-west of Grassington, in the valley of the River Skirfare; you can reach it along a minor road off the B6160, going left after passing Kilnsey Crag. Sat nav: BD23 5QJ.

Parking: Park outside the inn.

Pastoral and gritty, Littondale – the 'Queen of the Yorkshire Dales' – has hardly changed in five millennia, evidence of Bronze and Iron Age settlements abounding. Gathered around the crystal-clear Skirfare, Litton's ancient cottages breathe repose, its crags and heather-clad hills tugging at impatient boot strings. This is one of the remotest and most stunningly beautiful valleys in the county.

This is a relaxing walk by the River Skirfare, which flows along fissures in the porous limestone rock. Watch out for rising trout and grayling, and for water birds such as the yellow wagtail and the dipper.

THE PUB THE QUEENS ARMS is a captivating little 17th-century inn. Thirty years ago I supped well, stayed overnight, wet a fly and wondered if I would ever return. After a few difficult years, the pub was sold, and in 2012 its fortunes were revived with a sensitive refurbishment honouring its origins. And the place has its own microbrewery. This time I'll stay a month! A recent award winner, the inn serves traditional fare with a nod to the contemporary, and is popular with locals – it sells postage stamps and bread – and visitors alike, walkers, cyclists, fishers and artists all flocking to its door. Small and bijou, it can get a little crowded. There are six letting bedrooms.
www.queensarmslitton.co.uk ☎ 01756 770096.

The Walk

❶ Turn right from the inn along the road, passing **Litton Hall**.

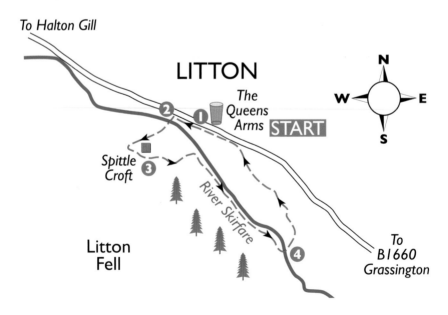

The River Skirfare

2 After around 200 metres, turn left, heading towards the river, and cross the bed of the **Skirfare** on a footbridge. Bear right across two fields to the back of **Spittle Croft**.

3 Turn left on a descending path to the river, and continue along the footpath signposted to **Arncliffe** for ¾ mile, to a point where a loop in the river ends.

4 Cross left here, and weave left on the well-marked footpath back to **Litton** and the inn.

Places of interest nearby

Visit **Kilnsey Park Estate** (see Walk 18).

Linton Falls near Grassington

20 GRASSINGTON

Distance: 2½ miles / 4 km

Map: OS Landranger 98 / OS Outdoor Leisure 2 GR: SE 003641

How to get there: Grassington can be reached on the B6265, which runs between Pateley Bridge and Skipton, or on the B6160, which runs north from Ilkley. Sat nav: BD23 5AQ (the Square) or BD23 5LB (Grassington National Park Centre).

Parking: Park in the Square (limited period only) or in the pay and display facility next to the National Park Centre, just south of the town.

Grassington, the 'gateway to Upper Wharfedale', is a crowded, craggy town of tall buildings set into the hillside overlooking Yorkshire's finest river. Despite the genteel tourist shops and smart restaurants, the surrounding countryside presents an enigmatic wilderness of rocks, abandoned medieval villages, field systems and the remains of the once-extensive lead mining industry. The extraction of the metal just a few miles up the road at Yarnbury, at the edge of Grassington Moor, once occupied hundreds of men.

This is a short, serene walk, passing Tom Lee's old forge and taking a back lane to the river and the beauty spot of Ghaistrill's Strid. Following the riverbank, the walk leads to the picturesque Linton Falls, beside an old mill, before returning along a quiet track and by back alleys to Grassington.

THE PUB THE BLACK HORSE is a 1650s coaching inn, thoroughly modernised and extended for the motor age. Standing foursquare in a prime position, it has stout quoins, a plain no-nonsense sign and a rearing facade. But inside, all is air, light and modernity, the inn having recently undergone an impressive refurbishment. A behemoth compared to some entries in this book, it offers 15 letting bedrooms and has the capacity to serve 100 restaurant diners, with some of the most imaginative food and drink for miles. www.blackhorsehotelgrassington.co.uk ☎ 01756 752770.

The Black Horse Hotel

The Walk

1 From the hotel, walk into the **Square**, and turn right and right again, going uphill on the lane past Tom Lee's old blacksmith's shop (now a florist's). In 1766, the foul deeds of Tom Lee came to national attention with the discovery of the murdered body of a local doctor in nearby Grass Wood. Lee was executed in York, and his body was gibbeted in what is now a nature reserve. Pass the library, and turn left down **Chapel Street**. Pass the **Methodist church**, and at the junction with **Bank Lane**, sweep left downhill, swinging right on the lane to the junction with **Grass Wood Lane**.

2 Turn right along this lane for 50 metres, and go left on a track, following the 'FP River Wharfe' sign; swing right towards a barn. Go through a gate, and turn left at the barn to a fence and a wall corner. Go left through the wall gap, and follow the wall down to the river.

3 About-turn at the rocks, and go left along the riverside path towards the bridge, gradually bearing left and going through a kissing gate to the road. The packhorse bridge was erected in 1603. Although most of the bridges over the Wharfe have, at one time or another, been

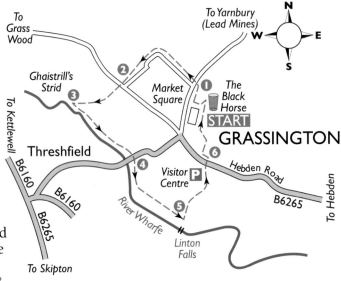

washed away by floods, this proud structure has remained solid.

4 Cross the road, and go left for 20 metres; then turn right, following the sign 'FP Hebden and Burnsall'. Continue along the riverbank, and cross a footbridge over a stream, swinging left past the first weir to the second weir.

5 Go through a wall gap, and follow the path left, signposted 'To Grassington Village', on a causeway. Continue, and go left through a gate into the **National Park Centre**, crossing to **Hebden Road**.

6 Cross the road and go left, turning right up **Springfield Road**. Go left at the end, and turn right on the path. Go next left, and weave left back to the square and the hotel.

Places of interest nearby

Take the dead-end road north-east from Grassington signposted to **Yarnbury** to view some of the best-preserved lead mining industry remains in the country. Information boards point out the main features.

In Grassington's Square, housed in two former lead miners' cottages, is the volunteer-run **Grassington Folk Museum** (www.grassingtonfolkmuseum.org.uk), which depicts local life, including the area's mining heritage.

Countryside around Burnsall

21 BURNSALL

Distance: 2½ miles / 4 km

Map: OS Landranger 98 / OS Outdoor Leisure 2 GR: SE 033613

How to get there: Burnsall lies on the B6160 north of Ilkley; it can also be accessed from the B6265 west of Pateley Bridge. Sat nav: BD23 6BU.

Parking: Park in the inn car park or on the riverside and roadside verges.

Lying in the lee of Burnsall Fell, near a curvaceous bend in the River Wharfe, the beautiful village of Burnsall has a 12th-century church, scores of pretty cottages and an impressive five-arch bridge – originally built as a gift to the village by Sir William Craven, a local man who went on to become Lord Mayor of London. The bridge is the centrepiece of an impromptu summer lido; following frequent floods, it has been rebuilt many times.

This stroll begins and ends on Burnsall's parapets. The walk crosses the river on a flimsy wire-and-plank Indiana Jones-type contraption, and returns through pastures, enjoying a different view with every stride.

THE PUB THE RED LION was once a 16th-century ferryman's inn. Stone-built hard by Burnsall's picturesque bridge, it announces its solid and timeless credentials with the monolithic horse trough at the front door; inside, meanwhile, is a resident cellar ghost. A family-run

enterprise, the Red Lion Hotel and Manor House offers luxurious accommodation, including rooms and holiday cottages, and gourmet food. Field sports, including shooting and fly fishing, can be arranged.
www.redlion.co.uk
☎ 01756 720204.

The Red Lion

The Walk

❶ From the back car park of the inn, go left upstream along the riverside promenade, and continue through a series of gates for about a mile on a well-defined, well-signposted footpath to the pedestrian footbridge. The path passes a crag on the far side of the river known as **Wilfrid Scar**. St Wilfrid, Bishop of York, is said to have preached here prior to establishing his church in Burnsall in AD 700. Turn right over the bridge, and cross to the opposite bank.

❷ Walk on and go left through a gate; cross the corner of a field, going through a second gate and turning right on the lane. Cross the **Hebden Beck** on a bridge and go left, following the '**FP to Hebden and Bank Top**' sign. Continue between the bungalows; follow a path on the woodland edge through a kissing gate to another gate. Go through, and continue to the footpath signs to the right of the trout hatchery.

❸ Swing right on the ascending path for about 50 metres, following the sign to **Hartlington Raikes**. Fork left off the track before the gateway, looking out for a stepped walk crossing. Cross the wall and the apex of a narrow field, and go through a wall gap by the footpath sign, following the sign direction left over a field and heading for a big tree to the right of **Ranelands Farm**.

❹ Go through the gate, and cross the farmyard, swinging right; go through a second gate, veering left off the farm track and heading diagonally left uphill towards the field top corner. Go through the gate, veering right for 20 metres to the angle of the wall in the next field – look out for the footpath sign on the other side of the wall. Follow the sign direction, continuing uphill over a rutted track. At the brow, look out for a big tree at the field boundary, and walk to the right of the tree towards a footpath sign next to a wall. Go left here, ignoring the next gate opening and following the wall down to the corner. Cross right over the ladder stile, following the direction sign, and continue wallside for 120 metres. Go left over the second ladder stile, and follow the fence down for 250 metres to the third ladder stile. Cross, going diagonally left over a field to a direction sign.

5 Keeping in the field, arc right, and follow the field boundaries and the sign marked '**FP Burnsall ¾**'. Go through the gated wall gap, veering right and left at the tree to cross this second field. Keep diagonally right, and head just to the right of the field corner, going through a gated wall gap; follow the footpath sign into the narrow fourth field. Cross, and go through a wall gap into the fifth field, veering away from the descending wall to find a wall gap. Cross to the lane.

6 Cross the lane, and go through a wall gap, dropping down and veering right to a ladder stile. Cross, swinging right and left to the riverbank. Follow the wall down to a gated wall gap, and go through to the bridge, mounting the steps to the left and turning right back to the inn.

Places of interest nearby

St Wilfrid's Church is the oldest building in the village. It houses an original Norman font and has an inscription noting that the church was 'butified' in 1612 by Sir William Craven. This benefactor founded the Old Grammar School, which adjoins the church. The school building is now used as the local primary school.

Panoramic views near Appletreewick

22 APPLETREEWICK

Distance: 2½ miles / 4 km

Map: OS Landranger 98 / OS Outdoor Leisure 2 GR: SE 050602

How to get there: Appletreewick lies east of the B6160, which runs between Bolton Bridge and Burnsall. Turn off at Barden Bridge. Sat nav: BD23 6DA.

Parking: Park in the inn car park opposite the inn.

With its yeomen's cottages strung out like fruit on a bough, poetically named Appletreewick – Aptrick to the locals – sits quietly in the shadow of Whithill, attentively gazing towards a bend in the River Wharfe and beyond to Simon's Seat – one of my favourite Yorkshire hills. This tiny village was once a resting place for monks journeying between Fountains Abbey and Bolton Priory, and its Monks Hall or Mock Beggar Hall remains, together with a building – now the church of St John – that was the birthplace in 1548 of William Craven. Apprenticed to a mercer in London, Craven went on to become the capital's Lord Mayor, returning to Yorkshire to restore his family home.

This spectacular walk, using old lead miners' tracks, takes you from the village stocks to the panoramas of the high moors before returning alongside gentle riverbanks to the village. The gradients of the first ½ mile are slightly challenging, but the views are worth it.

THE PUB THE CRAVEN ARMS is a delightful 16th-century family-owned inn that oozes atmosphere and treasures from a bygone age. Its bar, snug and dining room radiate cosiness, log fires and gas lighting adding to the restful ambience. Even the toilets are a talking point: portraits of local celebrities and heroes fill their walls! The inn serves locally produced food and ale and offers overnight accommodation in attractive shepherds' huts. Alongside is a beautifully restored heather-thatched cruck barn that is available for hire. www.craven-cruckbarn.co.uk ☎ 01756 720270.

The Craven Arms

The Walk

1 Turn right from the inn for a few yards; just past the stocks, turn right again on the steep track signposted to **Dibble's Bridge**. Go through a gate, and swing right, continuing to the summit. Go left through a gate, swinging left and right on a wallside track, and veer left to the field corner, going through a gate.

2 Turn left on a track signposted to **Hartlington**, and continue to the barn; go right through a gate, following the footpath and bridleway sign. Where the walled track ends, keep following the single wall, weaving down right and then left to the bridleway sign. **Hartlington Hall** is across the valley to the right; its founder, Ketel de Hartlington, came over with William the Conqueror. In his eccentric will, his descendant Henry Hartlington, who died in 1467, left his 'soul to the omnipotent God and his body to the church of St Wilfrid at Burnsall'. Keep going forward downhill to the bridleway sign, and drop down on a sunken track to a stile, crossing to a lane. Cross and continue on

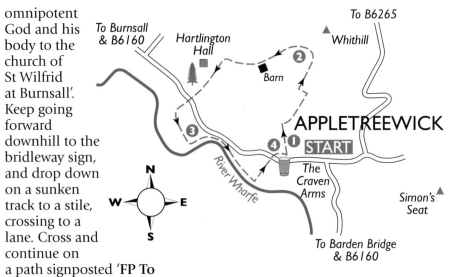

a path signposted 'FP To Dales Way Path'. Swing left, following a sign to **Appletreewick**, and go left of the farmhouse through a wicket gate, walking on through a gate by a barn and through a further gate, following a wall down to the riverbank.

❸ Turn left on the riverbank for about ¾ mile; at the '**Appletreewick**' sign, go left on a path between dwarf walls (this path is not shown on the OS map) walking on to the lane.

❹ Turn right along the lane, climbing back to the inn.

Places of interest nearby

Just five miles away are the **Stump Cross Caverns** (www. stumpcrosscaverns.co.uk ☎ 01756 752780). Discovered by miners in 1860, these 500,000-year-old caves contain a superb collection of stalactites and stalagmites, and remains of wolverine, reindeer and bison. There is a tea room, a gift shop and a lecture theatre showing a short film about the caves' formation. Hard hats provided. Open from spring to the end of November.

Winterburn Reservoir

23 HETTON

Distance: 4 miles / 6.4 km

Map: OS Landrangers 98 and 103 / OS Outdoor Leisure 2 GR: SD 963589

How to get there: Hetton is on a minor road between Gargrave and Grassington. The best access is from the east, using the B6265 and turning off at Rylstone. Sat nav: BD23 6LT.

Parking: Park in the car park opposite the pub.

With spectacular views of the fells, tranquil Hetton is an ancient farming community, its tracks providing some of the best walking country in the National Park. Such was its isolation that the parish once housed a fever hospital. With its closure in the 1920s, the village again reverted to relative anonymity, until its 600-year-old inn was revived to national acclaim.

This is a simple walk, with the path leading you along old tracks to the shores of Winterburn Reservoir, constructed between 1885 and 1893; the route returns over fields and along a classic green lane. Make sure you eat after your walk, because the marvellous food at the Angel will make you never want to leave.

The Angel Inn

THE PUB THE ANGEL INN is an award-winning pub that attracts customers like bees to a honey pot. The drovers who called at this wayside inn in the 15th century would surely have thought that they had gone to heaven. Timelessly English, with oak beams and open fireplaces, the Angel provides a miracle for the booted classes: where else can you sample such high-standard fare and some of the best ale in the county in your walking socks? The inn has nine letting bedrooms. www.angelhetton.co.uk ☎ 01756 730263.

The Walk

❶ Turn left from the inn, walking along the lane for about 150 yards, and go left, following the bridleway sign to **Hetton Common** along a track – **Moor Lane**. Go through a gate and continue along a track, climbing steadily for just under 1½ miles. If you're feeling adventurous at this point, the moorland track ahead over **Hetton Common** leads to the magnificent **Gordale Scar** and **Malham Cove** (see Walk 24).

❷ At the gated access to the moor, turn left, following the 'BW Winterburn' sign and going through a gate over a rough field towards **Alans Plantation**. Go through a gate into the wood; leave the wood through a further gate and cross the pasture land, steering left, going through a gate, and keeping straight forward towards **Long Hill Farm**.

3 Go through a gate and keep the same direction, passing the farm fenceside to arrive at the field corner.

4 Go through a gate, and follow the signpost left over a very large field. The path is indeterminate for the next ½ mile, so look out for a long wall on the left – you need to keep left so that you gradually converge with this wall. Keep well left of the right-angled wall to your right, and drop down towards the field corner, swinging right to a gate.

5 Go through, and turn left over the small field to the corner; go left again through the gate along a green lane towards the farmhouse.

6 At the corner, turn left along **Cross Lane**, going through various gates to rejoin **Moor Lane** and retrace your steps back to the car park.

Places of interest nearby

Nearby **Skipton** has a wealth of attractions, including the 900-year-old castle (www.skiptoncastle.co.uk ☎ 01756 792442), one of the best preserved in the country. Daily tours.

Also in Skipton is the **Craven Museum & Gallery** (www.cravenmuseum.org ☎ 01756 706407), its displays including items relating to the social history of the Dales.

Close by is **Rylstone**, which has a rustic pond and, hidden from view, a picturesque church. Rylstone is the setting for Wordsworth's poem *The White Doe of Rylstone*.

Malham Cove

24 MALHAM

Distance: 4 miles / 6.4 km

Map: OS Landranger 98 / OS Outdoor Leisure 2 GR: SD 903628

How to get there: Malham, east of Settle, is best accessed from the south by turning off the A65 west of Skipton and driving through Airton and Kirkby Malham. Sat nav: BD23 4DB.

Parking: Park at the pub or in the pay and display visitor centre car park.

Geology in Malham takes star billing: the grandeur of its limestone canyon, its waterfalls and its characteristic pavements, with their clints and grykes, have drawn visitors for centuries. Straddling the banks of the Malham Beck, a brawling infant that issues from the amphitheatre of the fantastic Malham Cove, this ever-popular village is a rambler's paradise. Much of the wild and exceptionally attractive surrounding countryside has been secured for the nation by the National Trust. Such is the route's reputation as the most scenic in the county that its omission from any explorer's itinerary would be unthinkable.

The walk approaches the portals of the gigantic Gordale Scar before climbing to the most impressive natural spectacle in the whole of Yorkshire. A 300-foot high, billion-ton slab of riddled and fractured limestone embracing a puny beck, Malham Cove has terrifying cliffs and an overwhelming enormity that is more than the craning neck can comprehend. Crossing the deeply fissured limestone at its summit

– look out for the rarest of flowers – you'll return by steep paths, following the beck to the village. Good boots, sure-footedness and a head for heights are all essential for this route.

THE PUB THE LISTER ARMS is a thoroughly modernised 18th-century coaching inn that preserves an old-world charm. Exposed stonework and wood, cosy niches, alcoves and log burners in winter create the perfect retreat after rugged days on the hills. Just one mile from Malham Cove, its en-suite accommodation includes walking guides and facilities for airing muddy boots! In this wildest area of Yorkshire,

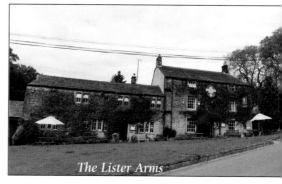
The Lister Arms

appetites are finely honed; the inn has a particularly good reputation for wholesome and satisfying pies.
www.thwaites.co.uk/hotels-and-inns/inns/lister-arms-malham
☎ 01729 830444.

The Walk

1 Turn right from the inn along **Finkle Street** to the junction with **Cove Road**, and turn left, passing the **Buck Inn**. Continue for 20 metres, and turn left over a footbridge signposted to **Janet's Foss**. Continue through a gate alongside the beck, going left then right through a wicket gate and keeping on the broad and well-defined track. Go through the next wicket gate and follow the '**FP Janet's Foss**' sign left for 100 metres wallside to the barn. Go left over the ladder stile and turn right, following a wall to a wicket gate. Go through, following the yellow arrow marker right to another wicket gate; go through and continue on a track wallside. Cross a ladder stile, and continue beckside to a further ladder stile, crossing into the National Trust reserve of Janet's Foss. In every man and woman there is a sooty imp itching to get out: here is the perfect opportunity to imitate the chimney sweep hero in Charles Kingsley's *The Water Babies*, who was inspired by this wonderful place. Continue to the left of the foss, and go through a wicket gate to the lane.

2 Turn right down the lane for 250 metres to **Gordale Bridge**. Go left, following the sign to **Malham Cove** over the pasture. Go through a wicket gate, and follow the wall up to a second wicket gate; cross into a second field, and go right up some steps to a further wicket gate, swinging left wallside on a track. Go through the next wicket gate, swinging right towards the lane and following the lane wall to the right for 200 metres to the signpost.

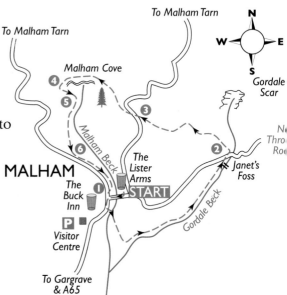

3 Go through the wall gap to the lane, and turn right for 10 metres; then go left over a ladder stile, following the signpost to **Malham Cove**. Steer right on the broad track wallside to the marker post, and veer left following the signpost, swinging right to a ladder stile and left across the limestone pavement at the top of Malham Cove.

4 At the end of the pavement, weave left to a ladder stile, and cross left down some steps, weaving steeply down right and left through two gates to the bottom.

5 Turn right on the broad path, and continue through two gates to the lane – **Cove Road**.

6 Turn left into the village, and go left at the junction with Finkle Street back to the inn.

Places of interest nearby

No visit to Malham is complete without a visit to **Gordale Scar**. In 1808, William Turner produced a magnificent, brooding portrait of this natural wonder. Also worth a visit is **Malham Tarn**, the second largest natural lake in Yorkshire.

Warrendale Knots near Settle

25 SETTLE

Distance: 4 miles / 6.4 km

Map: OS Landranger 98 / OS Outdoor Leisure 2 GR: SD 819637

How to get there: Settle is located on the A65 Skipton–Kendal road. Sat nav: BD24 9EF.

Parking: Park in the centre of Settle (in the Shambles) or in the pay and display facility 300 metres north-west of the town, near the railway viaduct.

Squeezed into the neck of Ribblesdale, with rough rock scars outreaching its chimneys, Settle is a frontier town where you check your ammunition before setting out into the unknown. Still a bustling place, the town is clustered around its Shambles, a sort of rustic piazza. Other curious buildings, like the 17th-century Folly and Ye Olde Naked Man Café, also excite visitor interest. Set beneath the frowning Castleberg Crag, the town has long been identified with the surrounding scars and caves.

This memorable walk takes you to the famous Victoria Cave. Discovered in the year of Queen Victoria's coronation, it has yielded mammoth, elephant, hippopotamus and hyena bones, together with human deposits from the Stone Age. This fairly taxing walk reveals petrified seas of limestone, one of the typifying features of this part of the Yorkshire Dales.

THE PUB THE LION offers 14 stylish bedrooms and a restaurant and bar serving locally sourced, seasonal fare. Built around 1640 as a coaching inn, the Lion is centrally placed in Settle, just a stride from the Shambles. Owned by the local Thwaites brewery, it positively welcomes walkers. www.thwaites.co.uk/hotels-and-inns/inns/lion-at-settle ☎ 01729 822203.

The Walk

❶ Turn right from the inn to the **Shambles**, walk across the parking area, and go right up the steep **Constitution Hill**. At the top of the hill, go left by the telegraph pole numbered 463722 and follow the track between the drystone walls, climbing up to a narrow copse. Go through a gate by a roofless barn, and continue wallside for 150 metres.

❷ Go right, following a public footpath sign to **Malham**, and climb steeply uphill wallside. Veer left, away from the wall, and continue, ascending on the green track to the right of **Blua Crags**. Go through a gate opening, and keep wallside on the flat path, noting the caves in the crags to the left. Pass the caves, and keep following the wall, continuing and veering left on a grass track. Cross a ladder stile and, keeping wallside, follow the path signposted to Malham.

❸ Swing left at the intersection of tracks, ignoring the right fork to Malham, and continue between the scars, climbing up over the limestone debris to the ladder stile to the right. Cross right and go left wallside, gradually veering right to the foot of **Attermire Scar**. Continue wallside, weave up right, and go through a gate; keep wallside on a

track, passing **Victoria Cave**. A scrambling path leads up to its mouth, where there is an information board about its history. As well as mounds of prehistoric animal bones, the cave has also yielded beads, brooches, fish harpoons, pottery and Roman coins. Walk on for about 400 metres, and go left through a kissing gate, swinging left to the 'Victoria Cave' sign.

4 Go left through a gate on a track, swinging right, left and right again alongside a wood to the road.

5 Go immediately left on the bend through a gate, following the '**BW Settle 1¼**' sign. Keep on the green track below the wood, and drop down right towards a copse. Go through a gate, continuing on a stony track to a second gate, and go through along a green track, dropping down to a third gate. Go through and follow the wall down, continuing through a fourth gate to rejoin the outward route. Follow this back to **Settle** and the inn.

Places of interest nearby

The countryside around Settle is arguably the best area in the world for fell walking, the incomparable **Three Peaks** triumvirate of Penyghent, Whernside and Ingleborough beckoning intrepid walkers to climb the famous trio in one hard day's outing. The town is also the HQ of the equally celebrated **Settle–Carlisle Railway** (www.settle-carlisle.co.uk), with steam engines regularly taking passengers on trips of a lifetime.

Giggleswick Scar

26 GIGGLESWICK

Distance: 3 miles / 4.8 km

Map: OS Landranger 98 / OS Outdoor Leisure 2 GR: SD 813641

How to get there: Giggleswick is a neighbour of Settle, just off the A65 Skipton–Kendal road. Alternatively, arrive by train. Sat nav: BD24 0BE.

Parking: Park in the inn's rear car park, or use the area at the Rathmell road junction, first left past the church going west (Raines Road).

With its own railway station, a distinguished public school, a trunk road passing its front door and the whole of glorious Ribblesdale on its doorstep, 'Gigel's village' has much to commend it. Built around the church of St Alkelda, which has a market cross outside its gate, it has a gaggle of interesting date-stoned cottages clustered around the Tems Beck. The village is internationally known for its excellent school, founded in 1553.

 This Dales foray along part of the Ribble Way takes you to the hamlet of Stackhouse and back along the foot of scree slopes crowned with intriguingly named features like Kelcow Caves, Nevison's Nick and Schoolboys Tower.

THE PUB THE BLACK HORSE is an appealing old coaching inn dating from 1663. Such is its proximity to the village church and its ecclesiastical architecture that you might expect only communion wine at this establishment. But fear not: it dispenses good cheer and traditional, locally sourced food in its twin bars and small dining room, gleaming copper and brass and an often-played piano giving it a homely feel. ☎ 01729 822506.

The Black Horse and Saint Alkelda's Church in Giggleswick

The Walk

1 Leaving the front door of the inn, walk towards the village cross and go left, turning left again up **Belle Hill** to the B6480. Cross the road and go right on the footway, walking on past the swimming pool towards the river bridge.

2 Just before the bridge and the '**Settle**' sign, go left on a path, swinging left riverside along the topside of the playing field. Keep arcing left for about 60 metres between a wall and a fence, and go right through a wall gap, crossing a meadow to a second wall gap. Go through, continuing wallside on a bank; cross a fence, and mount some steps. Keep forward fenceside to a wall gap. Go through into a meadow, and veer diagonally left to a gated wall gap and a sign.

3 Cross the lane; go right for 10 metres, and then left through a wall gap into a sloping field for about 20 metres. Swing right, following a line parallel to the lane towards the bottom of the wood. Converge with the wall on the right, and fork left uphill on a track, following the sign to **Feizor**. Keep climbing to the '**Stackhouse Lane/Feizor**' sign, and follow the Feizor route left, walking uphill and on over a field to a ladder stile. Do not climb the stile; instead, go left along the wall for 130 metres. Just west of here is the impressive **Giggleswick Scar**. These precipitous limestone crags are part of the **Craven Fault**. At the foot of the scar is the curious site of the **Ebbing and Flowing Well**.

④ Turn left at the next ladder stile, and cross the field corner, heading for the topside of a wood and following the wall down to a third ladder stile. Cross right and go left on a path, veering away from the line of the wall. Continue through the bracken, dropping down on the broad, snaking path, and go through a gate, swinging left to the wood. Go left through the gate into the wood on a track and drop down, continuing on a path into the residential area. Keep going forward on **The Mains** to the road. Turn right, cross the B6480, and go left back down **Belle Hill**, turning right to return to the inn.

Places of interest nearby

Go into Settle and turn left on the B6479 towards Horton-in-Ribblesdale to reach the **Watershed Mill Visitor Centre** (☎ 01729 825539). Based on a refurbished 19th-century cotton mill, it encompasses a range of stores selling outdoor clothing and footwear. It also sells real ale and whiskies, and has a coffee shop.

Embsay steam railway

27 EMBSAY

Distance: 3½ miles / 5.6 km

Map: OS Landrangers 103 and 104 / OS Outdoor Leisure 2   GR: SE 008538

How to get there: Embsay lies north-east of Skipton, one mile from the A59 bypass. Sat nav: BD23 6RA.

Parking: Park in the pub's rear car park or in the adjacent free car park along the road to the right.

This old mill town is dominated by Embsay Crag, whose shadow once fell on an Augustinian priory, founded here around 1120. On the very edge of the Yorkshire Dales National Park, it is the gatehouse to thousands of acres of moors and fells with captivating names like Punchbowl and Ladle, Deer Gallows Ridge, the Whams, Onion Hill and Dolly Rogin, its position exuding something of the air of a rainforest clearing.

Using quiet lanes and paths, this walk takes you to the top of Embsay Crag, where you will enjoy panoramic views, before returning to the town alongside a reservoir and an old mill goit.

THE PUB — THE ELM TREE INN has been a popular local hostelry since the 17th century. Situated opposite the eponymous tree in pretty Elm Tree Square, this stone-built pub has spacious bars and dining areas, and has a good reputation for wholesome, well-cooked food and locally produced ales. It is a favourite haunt of residents, walkers, cyclists and visitors to the nearby steam railway. Two letting bedrooms are available.

The Elm Tree

www.elmtreeinn-embsay.simplesite.com ☎ 01756 790717.

The Walk

❶ Turn left from the pub, and go left through the car park and through a gate, crossing a field to the corner. Go through a wall gap, and turn right on a path, going through a second wall gap and diagonally left over a second field to the corner. Go through a kissing gate to the lane.

❷ Turn left using the footway, and pass the church of St Mary the Virgin. At the churchyard corner, cross the road to the right.

❸ Go through a wicket gate, following a footpath sign; cross two fields, going through a final gate and swinging left to the lane. Turn left for about 300 metres.

❹ Turn right uphill, following the bridleway sign to **Embsay Crag**. Cross the cattle grid and swing left, climbing up to the buildings at **Boncroft** and going left through a gate, following the bridleway sign. Pass **Milking Hill Wood** on the left and continue, ascending to a gate.

5 Go left through the gate, following the sign and blue-tipped posts along the well-defined path through the bracken, weaving right and left and up to the top of the crag.

6 Drop rightward off the crag and descend, gradually swinging left towards the dam wall. Fork right to the blue-tipped post, heading for the top of the reservoir, and fork right again, dropping down to the reservoir boundary wall.

7 Turn right wallside, cross the bridge, and swing right to the signpost, going left on a path to a stile. Cross and turn left on a track passing the reservoir to the sailing club.

8 Turn left on the lane (a no through road with few vehicles), and swing right by the waterworks, going left around the next bend alongside the goit ponds. Continue on **Pasture Road** back to the pub.

Map labels: Moors, Embsay Crag, Embsay Moor Reservoir, Water Treatment Works, Milking Hill Wood, The Elm Tree, Boncroft, Eastby, To Barden Bridge, START, P, EMBSAY, To Harrogate, Embsay & Bolton Abbey Steam Railway, Quarry, A59, To East Marton, To Skipton, To Addingham

Places of interest nearby

Opened in 1981, the **Embsay & Bolton Abbey Steam Railway** (www.embsayboltonabbeyrailway.org.uk ☎ 01756 710614) operates from the town, with steam engines *Illingworth*, *Beatrice* and *Norman* hauling regular services throughout the year. The railway runs a host of seasonal events.

Bolton Priory

28 BOLTON BRIDGE

Distance: 2 miles / 3.2 km

Map: OS Landranger 104 / OS Outdoor Leisure 2   GR: SE 071531

How to get there: Bolton Bridge, near Bolton Abbey, is just off the A59 Harrogate–Skipton road. Sat nav: BD23 6AJ.

Parking: Park in the hotel car park or in the pay and display facility north of the hotel.

Bypassed and made redundant by a rerouted A59, the old Bolton Bridge melts into a landscape made famous by Turner. The centrepiece of this walk is Bolton Abbey, a now-skeletal Augustinian priory and the subject of a number of Turner's beautiful paintings.

A simple amble that in dry weather can almost be accomplished in carpet slippers, the route follows both banks of the Wharfe to Bolton Abbey. Founded in 1151, the priory is raised on a promontory above a delectable sweep in the river, the rapturous eye rising in a symphonic cadence of views from its scalloped capitals to the wooded crags above the river and beyond to the moors and glens of Barden Fell.

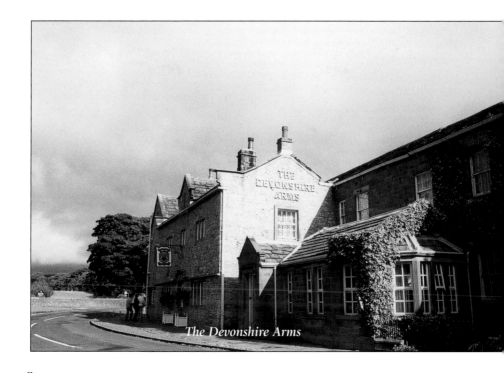

The Devonshire Arms

THE PUB THE DEVONSHIRE ARMS is a prestigious four-star hotel and spa complex set in a wild and romantic 30,000-acre estate in Upper Wharfedale. Owned by the Duke of Devonshire, it offers award-winning cuisine in its elegant restaurant and bars. If you can, stay awhile and revel in a series of patrician walks from the front door, taking in the famous cataract known as the Strid, the beguiling Valley of Desolation and the hilltop redoubt known as Simon's Seat. www.thedevonshirearms.co.uk ☎ 01756 701441.

The Walk

1 Turn left from the hotel, and walk on the footway following the closed road to the old bridge. Turn left onto the water meadows, following the signpost 'FP Bolton Priory'. Follow the path left towards the priory, which was dissolved in 1539, and explore the ruins (free admission). There is an interpretation board in the grounds. Drop down to the bridge and cross.

2 Swing left, and go right up the steep bank to the footpath signs, turning right on the cliff track signposted to **Bolton Bridge**. Go left over a stile, and continue beside the fence, turning right over a stile into a second field. Follow the fence down, going right and left downhill to another stile. Cross, and follow a footpath sign into a third field over a ditch. Go through a gate into a fourth field, and follow the path left uphill, veering to the right of next gate entrance, crossing a stile into a fifth field and swinging right fenceside to the right of the barn. Cross a stile, and walk on between the buildings to the road, turning right to the old bridge. Cross and return to the hotel.

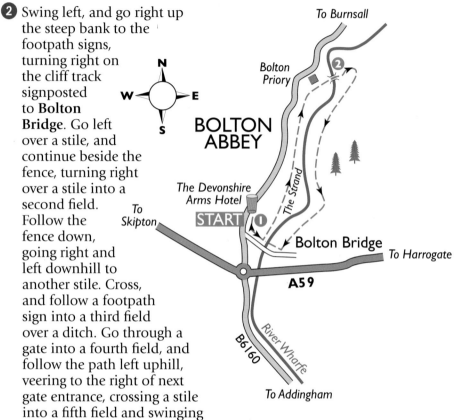

Places of interest nearby

Just up the road is the **Bolton Abbey Estate** (www.boltonabbey. com ☎ 01756 718000), which has a shop, a café and riverside nature trails suitable for children. A car parking charge is payable.

Panoramic view down Nidderdale

29 MIDDLESMOOR

Distance: 7 miles / 11.3 km

Map: OS Landranger 99 / OS Outdoor Leisure 30 GR: SE 092742

How to get there: Middlesmoor is the last village in Nidderdale and is around eight miles north-west of Pateley Bridge (B6265) on a minor road that follows the river upstream. Sat nav: HG3 5ST.

Parking: Parking is limited in front of the inn, but there is a free car park 200 metres to the north of the village.

The hilltop village of Middlesmoor occupies a lofty 900-foot-high perch at the top of Nidderdale. With a stone-built cluster of huddled cottages, cobbled yards and a church that has some of the finest views in England, it enjoys the magical reality of leading to nowhere, the scenic 'Yellow Brick Road' from Pateley Bridge ending abruptly at the moor's edge. 'These roads I would indicate on my secret maps by means of golden arrows,' noted my muse A. J. Brown in 1931, 'to let the Elect know that they lead to Paradise.'

The Crown Hotel

THE PUB THE CROWN HOTEL is described in brief and laconic Yorkshire fashion as 'the pub at the top o' the hill'. And what a hill! Surveying the whole of the valley, with Gouthwaite Reservoir twinkling in the distance, this 17th-century inn is a redoubt, the succour, in days of old, of farmers, drovers and builders who came here to construct the high dams at nearby Angram and Scar House. Today, this family-run inn provides bed and breakfast accommodation, a holiday cottage and a campsite. Like its thick walls and roaring fires in winter, the homemade fare and locally brewed ales are welcoming and warming. Walking sticks made by a local craftsman are on sale in the bar. www.crownhotelmiddlesmoor.co.uk ☎ 01423 755204.

The Walk

❶ Turn left from the inn, and go left on the ascending track, leaving the village and passing the car park to the right. Walk on for about two miles, crossing the moorland and heading for the distant dam of **Scar House**. Follow the zigzagging track downhill to the reservoir shore, turn right by the **Yorkshire Water Authority** building to the right, and go left after 30 metres, opposite the dam wall. Cross the dam on the footway.

❷ At the end of the footway, turn right, following the left bank of the **Nidd**. Pass the **Manor Farm** buildings and **Woodale Cottage**, and keep forward to **High Woodale Farm**, passing between the buildings. Go through a gate into a field, and steer left towards a gate near the left-hand top corner. Go left through it, and keep right, following the wall to the corner.

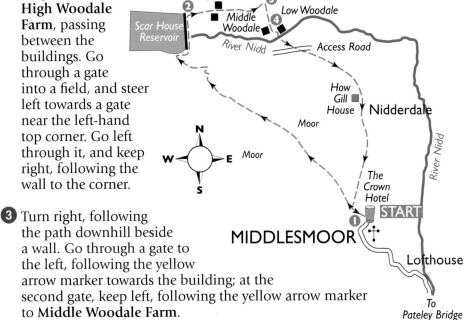

❸ Turn right, following the path downhill beside a wall. Go through a gate to the left, following the yellow arrow marker towards the building; at the second gate, keep left, following the yellow arrow marker to **Middle Woodale Farm**.

❹ Turn right across the cattle grid on a track heading away from the buildings, and cross the **Nidd**, walking uphill away from the valley up to a metalled access road. Cross the road, and swing left, passing **How Gill House**; gradually swing right, passing **Northside Head**. Keep on until the track merges with the outward route above **Middlesmoor**. Turn left back into the village.

Places of interest nearby

St Chad's Church (www.thechurchinthedale.com) was built on the site of a much earlier building in 1866. In a video posted on the church website is a fascinating, grainy, black-and-white 1930 short film showing the construction of the Scar House Reservoir.

How Stean Gorge (www.howstean.co.uk ☎ 01423 755666) offers caving, rock-climbing, canyoning and canoeing experiences under expert tuition. There is also a modern campsite, bunkhouse facilities and a café.

Ruin of Prosperous lead smelting mill at point 5

30 WATH

Distance: 8 miles / 12.9 km

Map: OS Landranger 99 / OS Outdoor Leisure 30 GR: SE 146678

How to get there: Wath is two miles from Pateley Bridge and the B6265, and can be accessed by minor roads that run north-west along both sides of the river. Sat nav: HG3 5PP.

Parking: Park in the hotel car park.

The hamlet of Wath ('ford' in Old Norse) and the surrounding acres were once owned by Fountains Abbey and the Archbishopric of York, sheep rearing and soaring profits from the woollen trade funding many a pinnacle and tower. From the 16th century, the hamlet had a mill which produced, over time, milled oats, barley and wheat, woven flax and linen, and bobbins. A largely intact 1880 successor mill and its millpond remain. The ford was supplanted by a bridge in the 16th century, its curvaceous replacement surviving. At the time of the construction of the dams in the high dale, Wath had its own railway station!

This stirring and energetic walk on parts of the Nidderdale Way takes us to the hushed and beautiful banks of Foster Beck, a watercourse that was once ravaged by the evanescent lead mining industry. But nature has slowly reclaimed the area, with only ruins and spoil heaps remaining; my favourite bird, the dipper, now patrols the rills. The route takes us to the Nidderdale capital of Pateley Bridge before heading back to Wath along the river.

THE PUB THE SPORTSMAN'S ARMS is but a fly's cast from the banks of the River Nidd and Pateley Bridge. Reposing in a dell, it is one of the fabled little inns that Izaak Walton so poetically described in *The Compleat Angler*. Family owned, stone-built and ivy-clad, it has an inviting bar, suitably adorned with fishing rods and stuffed fish, and an exquisitely dressed restaurant serving gourmet food. The menu emphasises fresh produce, including locally shot

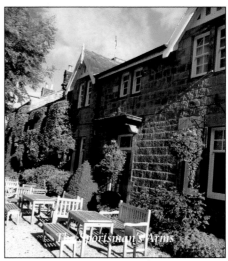

deer, grouse and other game. The inn has 11 en-suite bedrooms. www.sportsmans-arms.co.uk ☎ 01423 711306.

The Walk

1 Turn right from the hotel along the lane, and cross the hump-backed bridge over the **River Nidd**. Cross the road, and go through the gate into a field, climbing uphill left of the barn. Continue, climbing uphill over the gated fields, and keep to the left of the farmhouse, going right through a gate and passing the weather station to arrive at a track. Turn left to the lane.

2 Turn right along the lane for about 200 metres to the **'Foster Beck'** sign.

3 Go left on a track, passing the **Leeds Boys' Brigade** bunkhouse, and weave left uphill through a copse. At the summit, keep forward, walking fieldside to the right of a barn, and continue towards the farm buildings. Follow a blue arrow marker left between the buildings, down to the lane and **Foster Beck**.

4 Turn right on the lane, following the **'Ashfold Side Beck'** sign, and continue through the caravan park upstream, climbing gently towards the top of the valley for about ½ mile.

5 Just before the 'Private' sign, go left downhill, and cross the footbridge leading to the haunting and skeletal remains of the old Providence and Prosperous lead mines, the remnants of which are now scheduled ancient monuments. Between 1781 and 1889, these mines produced hundreds of tons of lead, the adjacent Greenhow Hill field producing thousands of tons more. Go left beckside, passing the archway, and walk uphill for 200 metres; swing right away from the beck on a looping track above the spoil heaps, following the 'Nidderdale Way' sign. Continue for around one third of a mile to the junction of tracks, and go left.

6 At the fork, keep right and descend on a rough track, swinging right over a cattle grid and going left uphill, passing **Hill End**. Walk on towards the distant **Pateley Bridge**.

7 Take the next signed left through a wall gap, and follow the wall down right and right again, going left to a kissing gate and through to Pateley Bridge. Turn right to the road, and go left over the river bridge.

8 Turn left down **King Street**, and keep forward along **Millfield Street**, going left into The Sidings. Follow the well-defined river and water meadows path upstream for about 1½ miles to Wath, and turn right back to the hotel.

Places of interest nearby

On the High Street in Pateley Bridge is the **Oldest Sweet Shop in England** (www.oldestsweetshop.co.uk), founded in 1827.

Around five miles east of Pateley Bridge is the 50-acre National Trust site known as **Brimham Rocks** (www.nationaltrust.org.uk/brimham-rocks), a landscape of wild moorland dominated by weather-beaten, monolithic rocks.
